Introduction to Patrick's Stories

An author who captures the diverse in his writings, Patrick K. Rocchio is consid be among the most entertaining America aut generation.

His original and personal stories are presented in a lyrical format which seems to create a "voice" by which he speaks directly and personally to each reader. No one is a distant stranger and every person becomes his close friend by experiencing the intensely personal emotions captured in Patrick's inspirational, often humorous, and always insightful stories.

In a sense, Patrick is you, the reader. His experiences become your personal experiences; his anecdotal stories become your anecdotal stories; his wry humor, his self-doubts, his simple joys, reflect an image of humanity easily recognizable by every reader as her or his own life story.

Skillful craftsmanship is displayed in the combination of language, mood, emotion, and thought that blend into a flow of words, syllables, accents, punctuation, and sentence structure which is a style associated with him, alone, in contemporary American literature. Patrick's writing style features a rare use of resonance, tone, and cadence, typically produced only in the playing of musical instruments rather than the author's voice expressed in two dimensional printed letters and words.

Patrick's life stories, indeed, describe the common threads of our distinctly human condition, sewn together into a seamless mosaic fabric that portrays the infinite variety of fascinatingly unique individuals which we, indeed, truly are!

Dedicated To All Caring People

It's Only a Name

I began my life and I have continued navigating the pathways of my life hindered by a set of rather odd or discombobulated first, middle, and last names.

My first name is Patrick, to honor my paternal grandfather, Pasquale Rocchio, consistent with Italian custom. My Mom, however, was not Italian and although she had a flexible and compromising disposition, she steadfastly refused to name her American born son Pasquale.

Apparently, she falsely persuaded my Dad (her spouse) that the English equivalent of Pasquale is Patrick, although there is no factual basis for that opinion. Actually, the English version of Pasquale is Easter; I am forever grateful that my first name is not Easter.

My middle name is unrelated to any aspect of the lives of my parents. They, reportedly, had no friend or acquaintance named Kent. It certainly is not a name with an Italian origin. I do believe today that my parents likely had intended a different name for my middle name when they had the name Kent inscribed on my formal birth certificate.

Rocchio is an appropriate surname or last name for me since that it is the surname or last name of my Dad. The problem is that Rocchio is deeply Italian and Patrick is a fabled Irish name, and, Kent has no ethnic significance whatsoever. So, what am I, ethnically speaking, anyway?

I do not like to be called Pat because I regard that as a feminine version of the name. Obviously, I choose not to be called Patty or Paddy, because I find most uncomfortable my accurate perception of the feminine gender association made with those alternative names.

In summary, I have no problems or uncertainties with regards to my DNA based gender but I prefer to emphasize my male identity in the form of my first name. My preference, therefore, is Patrick but should you call me Pat you will not be admonished or corrected by me. Just do not repeat or do it a second time.

Underwear on the Clothesline

My childhood and teen years were lived in a house located on the southwest corner of South Jay and East King Streets, in Kokomo's very middle class near south east side neighborhoods. Being a corner house, with the front facing east onto Jay street, the passing public was provided with an unimpeded view of the north side of the residence, including open absolute access to a cement patio, and the complete rear yard on the west side of the house.

During most of my youth we lived without the comforts of a modern washing machine and clothes dryer. Or, I should state, my Mom lived without the comfort of those household appliances.

Instead of popping soiled clothes into an automatic washer, then returning later to retrieve the load and transfer the wet bundle into an attached dryer, my Mom would toil weekly in the damp and unfinished basement and make do with what we could afford to master (tolerate) the challenging conditions of her life.

She was furnished with an antique era "spinner tub" to wash our clothes. After washing, she would run the dripping clothes through the ringer attached to the top of the washing machine, and then commence the task of drying our clothes by carrying them up the steps and outside in a clumsy and heavy metal tub or basket. That tub also did double duty as our improvised backyard pool.

Once Mom arrived outside with the damp clothes, this is where things got personal for me. Taking clothes pins from a bag, hanging on the stretched tight line made of thin beige colored cable, my Mom would remove the items of clothing piece by piece and hang them from top to bottom for public view.

That's full frontal nudity for my underwear. No creepy imagination necessary. No sicko window peeping required. Just look and see, people.

However, I never cared or had concern for the unveiling of my underwear (mixture of tighty whiteys and boxers) until the summer of 1963. In those times, it was the custom for driver training vehicles from the high school to practice basic driving skills by using the streets in my neighborhood in mid-June, July, and early August.

The first summer that included my classmates as student drivers was the year of 1963. Around and around all day cars would pass the exposed backyard of my house, on Mondays always and other days occasionally, and the occupants and classmates riding in those vehicles would have a clear view of my underwear bobbing and weaving on the clothesline.

Wait! There's more!!

In those times it also was the custom for the spirited high school band to practice its routines by marching around the streets of my neighborhood. This would occur every day like clockwork beginning in midsummer and continue until the week before the start of the new school year.

The effect of this marching band routine was to expose for unimpeded viewing by 400 added sets of curious teen eyeballs my then legendary underwear floating loosely on a clothesline in a soft afternoon wind on a breezy summer day.

During the summer months of 1963 I would frequently visit the dance hall at Seashore Pool on most evenings and interact with other students at the high school where I, too, was enrolled in a morning session summer driver's training course.

I suppose it was sitting in the back seat of a driver's education car passing the north side of my house when I first became aware of the underwear scandal which had developed on the clothesline strung across my backyard.

Or, it might have been when I noticed some girls looking at me and giggling in class during summer school, or smiling sheepishly and pointing me out to their friends at the pool's dance hall, or it might have been the laughter coming from the lowered back windows of the driver's training cars pausing momentarily to view my wind blown briefs, or the wide grins on the faces of the members of the marching band as they paraded past my dangling underwear.

I cannot remember how this crisis was resolved in my life. Perhaps, it took care of itself by the passage of time. In the early winter of 1964, my dad treated my mom to the purchase of a modern washing machine and, thankfully, a companion dryer for our clothes. She no longer had a need for use of the backyard clothesline.

I did, however, begin to miss that special fragrant aroma found only in an ivory white bed sheet and pillowcase dried on a backyard clothes line in the warm breeze of a beautiful summer day.

The Rocchio Family on South Jay Street

In early summer, 1939, in anticipation of his planned wedding to my Mom, scheduled for November 18, my Dad spent all of his after work hours constructing a house on a vacant lot he had bought at the corner of East King and South Jay streets. He was assisted by a friend who was a carpenter.

By the wedding day, the construction of the house had been completed and after a brief honeymoon to Chicago, my parents began living their life together, converting the house my Dad had built into a sentimental home for a family.

They never moved from that house at 701 South Jay Street, contentedly anchored to it during their marriage that lasted almost 70 years, until my Mom's death in January, 2009. My Dad continued to live in the house, alone, until his death in 2013. Indeed, at age 98, he died inside the house with tools in his hands when he apparently suffered a sudden stroke while in the course of completing a small interior repair job.

My Mom and Dad were loving parents to both my older sister, Jan, and me. They created an atmosphere of safety and comfort inside the walls of the house to which I was brought from the hospital soon after my birth in 1947. They made it easy and natural for their daughter and son to feel secure and safe inside our family home.

I never regarded our home as being a small, undersized, or claustrophobic inducing house. However, it certainly did have a small and awkward floor plan, requiring a person to walk through my bedroom to an adjacent bedroom occupied exclusively by my sister. The dimensions of the dining room lacked the space necessary to enable the table to be centered instead of being placed against a wall, thereby allowing us to just barely squeeze through into a hallway.

The master bedroom occupied by my parents was not a classic over-sized room noted for luxuriant accents. It, too, was very small in size, requiring the bed to be positioned at a diagonal direction, allowing for the minimum clearance required for placement of a single four drawer dresser for their joint use.

The square footage of the bathroom was less than the closet in my current bedroom. A person could stand in front of the sink and medicine cabinet with mounted mirror and then swivel around 180 degrees to face the toilet, ready for a man's aim and use without shuffling a foot forward or sideways.

The kitchen was compact. It was a tight fit to squeeze between the table and the cabinets, the built in stove, and the small oven. The refrigerator stood at an angle in a corner, and no more than four chairs could be placed around the steel legged table.

The living room was literally the room in which we lived when not eating, bathing, or sleeping. Of course, it, too, was relatively small and necessitated some creative thinking by my Mom in arranging the couch, chair, television, end table, and lamps to fit into a functional layout.

The rear of the house featured a cement patio, not enclosed, without privacy, and open to viewing by those walking or driving by on East King Street. The front porch featured a view of the top half and rooftops of a set of industrial buildings, then occupied by Cuneo Press.

At night, with my bedroom window opened in the summer to catch a breeze to remediate for our lack of central air conditioning, I would be serenaded by the repetitive cadence of punch presses operating at the Delco Radio plant, located at the end of South Jay Street.

I never felt any embarrassment about either the location or size of my home at 701 South Jay Street. I always regarded it as a very fine house. I approved its appearance and was proud that the house had been built by my Dad and occupied exclusively by my parents, my sister, and me. When friends visited, both boys and girls, I never felt the need to apologize for the size of my family's home, or offer any excuse for its tightly fitted rooms.

Indeed, until I departed Kokomo and moved away to begin my college life in late summer, 1965, I was for all intents and purposes clueless about social and economic class existing in my hometown.

I had never felt an awareness of being either superior or inferior relative to others, as measured by my Dad's blue collar income, his labor intensive job as a foundry furnace operator, our ownership of only one car, our lack of country club membership, or the fact that not one person in my extended family had attended college or earned a professional degree.

During the Great Depression, my Mom stopped attending high school after completing her sophomore year and began working a shift at Delco Radio. My Dad, an immigrant at age 17 from a village in Italy, had no formal education in America, and he never mastered the accent intricacies of the English language.

But, having served in the harshest battle conditions in World War II while assigned to General Patton's famed 3rd Army, there was never a need or reason for anyone to debate or to question my Dad's patriotism and loyalty.

In retrospect, I believe I am fortunate to have lived my younger years in a family home rooted in the neighborhoods of Kokomo's near south east side. The experience shaped the formative core of my character, my values, and my beliefs. It was, truly, a good family for me.

When the house sold in 2014 I discovered its interior size was 943 square feet. My present house has 4,256 square feet. Size has not increased my sense of happiness.

Songbirds

There is no other beauty in this world to match the splendor of a bird singing a song in the morning. How could it be that such a small creature is the source of such beautiful sounds that fill the air triumphantly, as the sun rises over the horizon to greet us at the start of a new day?

It is not possible to regard life on earth as sorrowful or sullen, or evil, or ugly, when we have the music of the birds to brighten our days. There is such variety in their songs, the hopeful glorious messages birds transmit to us by the pitch perfect melodies they share with us each day.

It is remarkable that birds are given this prized gift of music. It is only by natural talent, not as a skill acquired by hours of practice, that a bird has the capacity to captivate us, to impress us as its appreciative audience, by its unique and powerful music, performed in the format of a private morning symphony for each listener.

It seems that music sung to us by a bird on a branch in a tree is a form of prayer. The song birds are singing to us a reverent prayer of thanksgiving, a joyful prayer of hope, an inspiring prayer of faith, a prayer that proclaims to us that life is good.

The music of song birds teaches us that today is a gift freely given, not earned, an opportunity to see, to hear, to touch, to taste, and to love in a way different from all yesterdays.

Garage Cleaning

In a few more weeks, it will be time for the annual garage cleaning at my house. The floor of my garage begins to resemble a barren field located in a dust bowl as we proceed through May towards Memorial Day.

However, before the warm weather fun begins the garage floor must be swept, the debris or junk sorted, and the accumulated trash hauled to the curbside for later disposal. I always feel good about myself and life when I perform the perennial spring garage cleaning every year. Can you imagine the condition of my garage if I did not do this activity faithfully on an annual basis?

My usual modus operandi is to remove every item and object from the interior of the garage and place them in the driveway. Then I proceed to sweep vigorously and in the process manage to stir up from its hibernation the winter grime that has become encrusted on the floor surface. Then I use a garden hose to spray the floor and presto I produce what appears to be a newly poured concrete surface in my previously dirty garage floor.

Next, I examine and inspect carefully every item and object I have placed in the driveway. There always are a few unfortunate pieces of junk which are selected and left curbside for removal later in the week by my tax supported municipal services truck. I feel bad when I select something to discard, classifying it as junk, as if it has a personality or identity, hurt and offended by my insensitivity.

Most everything taken out of the garage gets carried, pulled, or pushed by me back into the garage when I decide I have had enough of this activity and want to do something else with my valuable time, like have a snack, take a nap, or watch a ballgame on television. Closure requires me to find a new location inside the garage for each item or object which had been removed by me from the garage only a few hours before.

There occurs in our lives moments of great achievement, those rare times when we know for a certainty that human life has purpose, meaning, and effect. I have never discovered those moments while cleaning the garage each spring but I will keep looking since it may be found somewhere in the dust, the junk, or the debris.

1232 South Jay Street

My first bicycle delivered paper route distributing daily the late afternoon and weekend morning editions of the *Kokomo Tribune* covered the entire length of Jay Street south of Markland Avenue. The typical subscriber count was 100 homes plus the Turner grocery store at the southeast corner of Virginia and Jay streets.

This was my paper route from age nine in late 1956 until early summer in 1961, a few weeks after graduation from elementary school at St. Joan of Arc and before my 14th birthday celebrated on July 1. When the paper route that included my house and the Jay Street neighborhood north of Markland Avenue suddenly became available my request to have it in place of my first route was approved by the paper's circulation department.

I continued delivering newspapers on my Jay Street route north of Markland Avenue until mid-spring in 1963, my sophomore year at Kokomo High School. My interest in participating with friends in enjoyable after-school extracurricular activities necessitated my discontinuing the delivery of newspapers.

I enjoyed having a newspaper route and delivering the paper to customers throughout the week. I developed a "special" friendship or familiarity with the household residents, bolstered by my visit to the front door of every home on Friday evening or Saturday morning to collect payment of the weekly subscription fee of forty cents, a quarter, dime, and nickel.

It would slow down and delay my bicycling on the sidewalk along the street delivering papers, but it was a part of my routine to stop every day at 1232 South Jay Street, lower the kickstand, take a paper in my hand, walk to and step up onto the creaky wooden plank porch, and continue to the weather worn front door, twist the knob to the left to open the door, and enter into the home of an elderly man, Perry Thomas.

It was a very old and poorly maintained house in which Perry resided alone, his spouse having died before my introduction to him. Perry was a "shut in" who lived cloistered within the walls of the house. He seemed to suffer from paranoia, and disallowed any visitor or person to enter his house, with the exception of me and a single living relative, a nephew who resided a few blocks away in a house on South Bell Street.

Perry limited his living space to a single room only, directly accessible upon entry through the front door. In that room he had located his unmade bed, chest of drawers, table with a lamp placed on it, and a rather musty odorous stack of old newspapers on the floor, preserved according to him for a future day to be browsed or read when the time seemed right to complete the task. Actually, I had no reason to believe that Perry was capable of reading the words printed in the newspaper.

After entering into Perry's private living space, I would advance into the only accessible adjacent room, the sparse and darkened kitchen. It was furnished with an old refrigerator and a small corner table lacking the accessory of chairs.

My daily routine was to remove a container of milk and a loaf of bread from the refrigerator, crumble a slice of bread into a cereal bowl, pour milk onto the pieces of bread in the bowl, grab a spoon, and deliver the meal to Perry, patiently sitting bedside in the next room.

I would remain until Perry had finished eating, only occasionally exchanging conversation, me a young boy and he an elderly frail man, two people who without this daily ritual meal would never have known of the other's existence.

After Perry had finished eating his dinner of crumbled pieces of white bread and cold milk served to him in a simple bowl, he would hand to me his bowl and his spoon to be carried by me back into the kitchen. There I would stand at the sink and wash the bowl and spoon, dry them, and place them on the table to be used for tomorrow's meal.

This daily ritual continued every day for the four plus years when I delivered papers on Jay Street south of Markland Avenue, on a route that included Perry's dilapidated house. After my route changed to the Jay Street houses located north of Markland Avenue I no longer visited or saw Perry. I introduced him to the boy who would be my replacement delivering papers on the route that included Perry's house, and I encouraged both to continue the daily routine I had established with Perry to provide him with the limited nourishment of an evening meal consisting of only bread and milk.

A few weeks after beginning the delivery of papers on my new route north of Markland Avenue, I asked the boy who had replaced me on my old route how Perry was doing adjusting to an unfamiliar person entering his house, preparing and serving his simple meal each day. Sadly, I was informed that after a few days Perry had refused to allow the boy who had replaced me on the route to enter his house and within two weeks thereafter he had died alone in his house.

Perry's lifeless and emaciated body had been discovered by his nephew who would occasionally visit the house to check on the status of his solitary uncle.

Today the land on which Perry's house stood when I visited him daily as his paperboy is a vacant lot. There is no longer a house standing at that address on South Jay Street. But, Perry Thomas still lives in my memory, and I am indebted to him for the joy he gave me by allowing me to prepare and to serve him daily a simple meal of crumbled bread and cold milk in a cereal bowl.

Kindness to others pays the provider the richest form of dividends. But, I do wish that I had returned to Perry's house to check on him after our simple meal routine stopped and I no longer had a reason to visit him on a daily basis. I hope that Perry died believing that a person did care about his welfare during his last years of his reclusive life, a young boy who saw behind the shroud of Perry's frail and aged body the glow of an eternal spirit.

Knock Out Flies

Danny and I often would play the game of knock out flies during summer vacation from school. Our favorite location was the grass ball field in the side yard directly south of the large red painted house located west of the Good Samaritan nursing home on East Vaile Avenue. It was occupied by the family of the man who was the general manager of the Kokomo Dodgers Midwest League team. We had an open invitation to use the lot to play baseball at all times.

In exchange for our informally granted permission-to-use license, Danny and I agreed that we would attend games at Highland Park and carry around our necks a canvas strap connected to a heavy tin container filled with bottles of cold soft drinks. For a dime a fan in the bleachers or grandstand could purchase a bottle of non-alcoholic liquid refreshment without hastily trotting to and from the general concession stand located behind the official scorer's wooden press box attached to a square shaped foundation of cement blocks.

By the end of every game Danny and I would be suffering from severe neck strain. But, we did earn a penny for each bottle sold and it was not unusual to finish the night with a quarter in my pocket. Danny and I rode our bicycles to Highland Park, for both day and evening games. Parents just assumed their children were safe on the streets in those days of less anxiety, stress, and worry.

Knock out flies was a simple game which required two boys to play it. If three or more played it was a different game than the simpler less competitive form played by Danny and me.

To begin, a wooden baseball bat would be tossed softly by Danny to me or from me to him and the recipient would catch it firmly with his dominant hand, his fingers wrapping tightly around the midpoint of the bat.

The boy who had thrown the bat would then place his fingers and the palm of his dominant hand tightly above the hand of his friend and this would continue in an alternative manner until a hand could no longer fit completely around the bat. The boy whose hand was last placed completely around the bat was declared the winner.

Winning met being the batter while the loser would grab his baseball glove and sprint out onto the field to await the ball to be hit to him.

The person hitting would throw the ball up in the air, ideally reaching shoulder height, grip the bat with both hands, then quickly swing the bat at the descending baseball, and with perfect eye hand coordination, hit it in the direction of the player standing with his glove in the field.

After the fielder caught cleanly 10 grounders, or 5 bouncers, or 3 fly balls, the roles would rotate and the batter would become the fielder and the fielder would become the batter and the cycle would continue for countless hours in the freedom of an unfenced and unscripted summer day.

Two young boys, both nine years of age, very best friends, experiencing life, together playing with a baseball, wooden bat and fielder's glove, a simple game of knock out flies.

Protecting Our Children

Following behind a school bus this morning, it occurred to me that we fail to express adequately to the capable drivers of those unwieldy oversized vehicles the gratitude we feel for their consistent daily performance of a job well done.

We can only imagine how difficult it must be to control the anxiety, to carry that burden of responsibility, being the sole person entrusted by both the parents and the community to protect the lives of the endangered children being driven on a large yellow bus to and from school each day.

It stimulates a recurrent surge of pride for me to see a bus passing on the road with the words identifying my local community school district printed conspicuously on opposite side panels and inscribed across the rear emergency exit door in solid black letters. A part ownership of that school bus is claimed by me.

It identifies our community's name, it is a symbol of our schools, it transports our precious children occupying the interior of that bus being driven to and from school. We expect that the person driving the bus is properly qualified, trained and skillful, attentive and prepared to react to the hidden perils waiting ahead on the road. We trust that he or she recognizes and appreciates that there is no greater treasure for us than our children and no greater concern for us than the assurance of their safety.

The perilous roads are now snow and ice covered, adding to the difficulty our school bus drivers encounter on their routes each weekday. This winter season we can acknowledge our respect for their indispensable service and applaud their skills by a display of patience and tolerance when we approach a school bus from its rear or encounter a bus slowing or stopping in traffic to complete the always dangerous process of children excitedly entering or departing a school bus.

Is there any occupation so under recognized as the brave drivers of our school buses? When you are sitting or standing next to a person you know to be a school bus driver, replace silence with your voice, and express on behalf of our entire community a few sincere words of thanks in recognition of a job well done.

Who is an American?

My Dad was born in a mountainous village in southcentral Italy, the youngest of nine children. At the age of 17, he departed from Naples, Italy, for the United States, traveling alone, on an ocean voyage on April 23, 1932, arriving at Ellis Island in New York harbor on May 2, 1932.

The year 1932 was the apex of the Great Depression. He spoke not a word of English. He had only a few dollars in his pocket. He had been given a note to explain that his destination was Kokomo, Indiana, where he had two brothers living and awaiting his uncertain arrival.

Somehow he managed to complete the journey to Kokomo. On June 15, 1939, he swore an oath of allegiance and became a citizen of the United States. Later, he was drafted by the United States Army and participated in combat operations in Europe in World War II assigned to General Patton's famed 3rd Army. He chose to remain on active duty in Europe for possible reassignment for the anticipated invasion of Japan, an act that delayed his discharge and return to America until midyear 1946.

My Dad had built his family's home at the corner of South Jay and East King Streets in Kokomo. He lived his adult life and he died inside that same residence while engaged in a home maintenance project at the age of 98, in 2013.

My Dad never discussed his World War II experiences until the final years of his life, when the memories were prompted from him by me.

He was most proud of his military service, telling me that it had anointed his American citizenship in such a way that no person could ever doubt my Dad's loyalty to country.

He was in every sense of the word an American.

Miracle of Nature

If you were a butterfly, you would appreciate how joyful it is to be able to fly from one flower to another. In its infancy, before it matures into a creature with wings a butterfly has no expectation of the life ahead. It is a remarkable discovery when the butterfly experiences its first flight of freedom through the air.

If you were a butterfly, you would enjoy the mist of a warm summer rain, the spectacle of colors splashed on the leaves of garden plants, and the sweet scent of pollen on the open petals of a flower.

If you were a butterfly, you would be amazed by the variety of plant life growing in the landscape garden bordering a house, the array of plant species populating the yard, the multitude of insects crawling on the leaves and branches of trees.

If you were a butterfly, you would find satisfaction in the common events of daily life, a brief moment shared with another butterfly, the warmth of an afternoon sun, the refreshment of a soft spring breeze.

If you were a butterfly, you would feel fortunate to be alive, to have the use of those aerodynamic wings fluttering in the wind, the brilliant colors decorating your body, the fulfilling task of pollinating plants in the cycle of life.

If you were a butterfly, you would be comfortable with whom you are, to accept your place in nature, to seek and expect the best from others, and to know by faith alone that in the blueprint crafted by intelligent design there is included a noble purpose to your being, both today and tomorrow in whatever form you may exist.

It is good to be a butterfly. It is more wondrous to be you.

Busy, Busy Me

When your mind senses that spark of inspired creativity, when you have that feeling that you are on the cusp of writing something profound and provocative, it is vital that you begin writing instantly, without any interruption, distraction or delay, transferring onto paper for the benefit of posterity those immortal words to be linked forever to your name.

This is that type of special moment. But first there is a call beeping, waiting impatiently to be answered on my cell phone.

It possibly could be a very important call, maybe a literary agent seeking to sign me to a lucrative contract, or national public radio inviting me to host a new weekly talk show, or perhaps a Hollywood screen writer seeking the exclusive film rights to my future first novel.

Before proceeding with my writing, let me check quickly the emails on my i-phone app to see if something has arrived since my last check of my message traffic.

It is always important to review every message to avoid the misfortune of deleting a message that might have been a really important message for me.

Concentration on writing seems an impossible chore to endure or task to complete without first securing reasonable assurance that my video player is set properly to record the entire last episode of my favorite television show, while simultaneously taping the replay of a classic 1984 World Series game, both to be broadcast later tonight, and on two different cable channels.

Likely, there is an instant message just waiting for my eyes to see, ready to command my fingers to type an instant response.

It could be important.

In fact, it is only described correctly as a type of instant communication because its importance demands both my immediate reading and my instant transmission of an equally significant and instantly important message sent as my instant reply.

What was that elusive spark of momentary inspiration that appeared in my mind at the beginning of this thread of wandering thought?

Suddenly and abruptly it has vanished, gone forever, evaporated, unplugged, released from the maze of those densely bundled convoluted language cells sleeping quietly now in my brain.

But, at least, I did not miss that cell phone call from whoever that was.

Every Life Tells A Story

Every person has a life that is full of stories. A mixture of successes, failures, accomplishments, and setbacks is the mosaic of human life. All of us have had our share of opportunities taken and opportunities missed.

Serving a dinner of beef stew, salad, and cold milk to a line of night time arrivals at the men's homeless shelter last week, caused my curious mind to wonder about the stories that accompany those lives.

What was that disappointment, or failure, or setback that brought each of them to this seemingly low point in his life, to this humbling humiliation, this moment of embarrassment, standing in line for a dinner handout, forced to sleep on a stiff mat on a cement basement floor in a charity sponsored homeless shelter on a freezing December night?

But, who are we to judge others? These men are not lesser men. Do we judge and value others by the measure of their material wealth or do we extend to all people the respect they deserve as members of our human family? It is not by the possessions he owns that we judge a man's value but by the person he is.

When they had finished passing through the serving line, I filled a plate and joined the others at a community table, mixing with them in their conversation, about the weather, about last night's football game, about politics, about the simple events of daily life. Just a group of men I sat with that evening at dinner. Not really any different from me.

Bang the Drum Softly, Please

At first, it must have seemed like a good idea. Parents were encouraging their children to "take up" the playing of a musical instrument. Until a student advanced to the 7th grade, the core curriculum in our public and parochial schools did not include the availability of a course in music.

Music education for the early elementary grades, therefore, was reserved for parental implementation. That being said, a child remained in a desert rather than an oasis of music unless the parents had either the money for formal lessons or the ability to play an instrument or carry a tune. My parents had neither in abundance.

Somehow Benny and Beulah located the money needed to enroll my sister, Jan, in a weekly private session with an accordion instructor. Why Jan agreed to the accordion will remain a forever mystery in my life. The "instrument" is large, heavy, and requires skillful use of both left and right hands.

In my preschool years, I had a red toy plastic trumpet. I do recall marching around the rooms in our house blowing loudly on that horn without producing any sounds that would be recognizable to a listening adult as pitch, tone, chords, or notes. It was just noise.

My parents had the good judgment to recognize that the sound of daily accordion lessons would equal their decibel limits. They had no intention of allowing me to add to the daily noise pollution by encouraging my "playing" of either a string or brass instrument.

So, they made the illogical choice of choosing the drums for their younger child. If that makes sense to you, please explain the logic to me. With a used snare drum bartered by my Dad in a trade with a co-worker, and set of drum sticks, I began attending weekly lessons taught by a professional drummer.

I continued with drum lessons for about 3 years until other school activities such as interscholastic sports forced cessation of my life as a drummer. I was never very good at playing the snare drum, anyway.

Actually, I never had the pleasure of playing a full set of drums. I never advanced beyond pounding a beat on my out of tune snare drum; a snare drum, incidentally, can be noticeably out of tune and my snare drum was so noticed by me although I am severely tone deaf.

Simply, my parents, constrained by a tight budget, could not afford to purchase a full drum set for me: snare and bass drums, a foot pedal, cymbals, the whole works. Besides, there was no space in my house for placement of a full set of drums and who would want to listen to the racket of my daily practice drills.

Someday I will purchase for my pleasure an entire drum set. I will assemble it in my home office in an area where the interior walls provide a sound barrier to the other rooms in my tranquil house. Whenever I choose I will sit on the stool behind my entire or complete drum set, lift the left and right hand sticks, and bang away until my arms become saturated by fatigue.

I always believed that I could have been an impressive drummer if I had continued with lessons during my early teen years. Possibly, I could have played in a garage band, featured at local dances, a desired date target for the prettiest girls in Kokomo. But, it never happened except in my imagination. Life would have been good to me as a drummer.

Setting The Pace of Life

Returning home in my automobile, while traveling in the western portion of Branch County on M-86, my progress was abruptly halted by the appearance of a tractor, pulling a planter, slowly moving ahead on the road in front.

Why are we in such a hurry to go from point A to point B? Why was it perceived, instinctively, as if necessary and required, for me to steer my automobile into a passing maneuver, press the accelerator, and burst past the slow moving tractor, chugging along otherwise as an irritating obstacle in my way?

And then that influential but usually silent "Let's do the opposite of what is expected of us" voice that resides in the back room of my personality spoke, and suggested with a subtle but persuasive appeal, that it might be better to follow the farmer on his tractor rather than passing around him.

This was an instructive moment, a learning experience, an encounter that forced me to consider that other influences rather than my agenda will decide in many situations how my life proceeds. There are times when a timetable other than mine may be the better plan for me.

After a few minutes following behind him, perched above me in the seat on his tractor, proceeding at a turtle's pace that he determined to be correct for us, the farmer arrived at his destination. He steered his tractor and the planter pulled behind it into the field on his right, disappearing into my peripheral vision as my vehicle moved ahead on the road.

Sometimes we need someone else to slow us down, maybe a farmer driving his tractor slowly in my path on a shared roadway, pulling the load of a planter, teaching me an important lesson about control, about the pace, about the choices made in my daily life.

Honor Your Patrick

Too many people in our community are unaware that St. Patrick's Day, celebrated annually on March 17, originated in our city, outside a cabin south of the Wildcat Creek, inhabited by the esteemed pioneer, Horace T. Phileas, the first settler who arrived in early 1842 and remained forever, intending to leave and travel westward by wagon only after weather conditions had improved.

This great day, now celebrated worldwide, was intended by Horace to be a day in recognition of a local person whose first name is Patrick, preferably joined with an ethnic surname, ending in vowels rather than consonants. It was on March 17, 1842, that Horace first opened the door of his cabin, looked out upon a sea of white snow, and exclaimed, "Pa tricked me" since it had been his father who had suggested that Horace travel westward in search of a homestead.

In the years following, after Horace met and married Harriet, his dear wife, and their children beget many children, the words first spoken by Horace were abbreviated to "Pa tricked" and soon thereafter combined for simplicity of speech into the single word Patrick. Since Horace is regarded as a saintly figure by those of us who claim this county as our home, we celebrate annually the day of his first emergence from his cabin hideaway as St. Patrick's Day, on March 17.

According to local custom, Horace declared before his death that the proper and only correct way to celebrate this glorious day is to identify a person in our beloved county whose name is Patrick, and express to him your respect, your love, your gratitude, for the gifts of his great life, his humble personality, his Hollywood star good looks, by doing an act of kindness in his honor, for example, purchasing and sending him a gratuitous gift card for the modest sum of Fifty dollars ($50.00) redeemable for a restaurant meal, a good book, car fuel, party snacks, golf balls, or just basic groceries.

Do what is right and just. Do it for Horace in memory of his courageous life and rugged pioneer spirit. Do it for a Patrick in your life. There must be someone, close or distant, whom you know named Patrick. Think about it.

Just An Ordinary Tree

It is always uncertain for me in winter, being a common or ordinary maple tree in a forest bordering a remote and distant farm, whether I will have in my future any leaves sprouting on my branches.

I dread this, appearing exposed in this terribly humiliating condition, without vegetation attached to my sprawling limbs, leaving me looking stark and foreboding to those who see me as I am, dull and dreary.

What if this never changes? In the past, winter always ends and gives way to spring and in the midst of warming weather my appearance has been transformed by the buds which burst forth into bright shades of emerald green.

Simply because it has happened before does not mean it will happen again to me. I cannot possibly be comfortable with this stressful anxiety tightened like a noose around me. Where is the certainty that I need in my life?

I never really chose to be a tree. And, if I had been given a choice, I would not have chosen to be located out here in an ugly forest, adjoining a remote farm, rooted into the ground, unable to escape from who I am.

Why is it not possible for me to be a tree standing tall in a robust city park, a playful family's backyard, or best yet, shading with my branches the landscape in a tropical climate controlled botanical garden, surrounded by a spectacular rainbow of colorful flowers and elegant shrubs?

It is unfair that I am a tree, without leaves, without any color but this dull bark on my trunk and limbs, trapped in this meaningless existence.

It should be my decision to be a tree, or a shrub, or a flower. What possible good is there in being a tree, placed in a distant forest, nearby an abandoned farmhouse, far removed from where I want to be, my future uncertain, having no reason to believe that leaves will sprout from these plain buds, without hope that my barren branches will be transformed by a decorative sprig of shiny green leaves?

Why did the creator of all things, seen and unseen, select this form of life for me? Is it good to be me?

Easter Lily

My formal name is Lilium longiflorum. I am a Bermuda lily, or as more popularly called today, an Easter lily.

My ancestral lineage or history can be traced to the Ryukyu Islands, which include the island of Okinawa, in the East China Sea. In North America, my bulbs are grown along the coast of the Pacific Ocean, near the border of California and Oregon.

After I was tenderly planted as a bulblet, I remained in the field for three years and required constant care and attention. As a mature bulb, I was harvested last fall, packed and shipped to a commercial greenhouse, planted in a pot, and placed under controlled temperature conditions to bloom for the Easter holiday.

We Easter lilies naturally bloom in the summer, but by use of special planting techniques, we can be programmed to bloom in the spring, to coincide with Easter.

Temperature is the magic potion used to speed up or slow down the appearance of our blooms.

I am called a "Nellie White," which is the name given to traditional Easter season lilies. My name originated with a grower, James White, whose wife was Nellie.

I am sure you have noticed that I have large, white trumpet shaped flowers. I am the symbol of purity, virtue, innocence, hope, and life.

I am mentioned numerous times in the Christian Bible. I am praised in the Sermon on the Mount. I am associated with the Garden of Eden, Holy Mary, the mother of Jesus, and the mystery of life everlasting.

I am proud to be me, and I am grateful that I have been created by my Creator to be a sign of beauty, a messenger of hope, a trumpet of joy, a beam of tranquility, an image of love. I am a lily of the field.

Rejoice and be glad. This day is made for you.

There is no past and there is no future. There is this day and it is your life forever more.

Carl Erskine

It is likely that all young boys have a hero. I was no exception to that near universal rule. During the 1950s in Kokomo my uncontested hero was a pitcher for the Brooklyn Dodgers named Carl Erskine.

About age six, in 1953, I was informed by my Mom that Carl was a distant cousin of my uncle, Jim Gerhart. He was married to my Mom's sister, Ruth, and they also lived in Kokomo. Uncle Jim was a very kind and thoughtful man; he attended my baptism and he was honored to have been chosen to be my godfather. Uncle Jim never forgot to recognize with fondness every milestone in my life by sending a greeting card or speaking with me on the telephone.

During the mid-1950s, Carl Erskine was enjoying his best years as a star major league pitcher. He had been born and raised in nearby Anderson, Indiana, and returned each offseason to his hometown.

In early January, 1957, in advance of the team's last year playing baseball in Brooklyn before its relocation to Los Angeles, a relative of my uncle Jim's died and the wake at a local funeral home was scheduled for the decedent's family members, both close and distant. Apparently, the deceased person also was related to Carl Erskine and it was known to my uncle Jim that my idol and hero would be in Kokomo and visit briefly the funeral home around noon on the scheduled day of the wake.

Uncle Jim requested my parents to allow him to take me with him during my lunch hour at school and go to the funeral home to see and to say hello to Carl Erskine. Of course, my parents agreed, and the day arrived when I rushed home, running the one block from the school to my house, to meet with my uncle Jim and drive to the funeral home for my viewing of Carl Erskine instead of the decedent.

As I opened and entered through the front door of my house on the east or Jay Street side of our corner home, I was startled to see not only my Mom and my Uncle Jim but also a man attired in a business suit. Yes, it was him --- Carl Erskine rising off the living room couch with his right arm extended to shake my hand!

This moment was the high point of my life to that day. Carl stayed at my house and ate lunch with me. He drank a glass of cold milk to encourage me to eat and to drink healthy foods and beverages. He graciously allowed me to wear his 1955 World Series championship ring on my finger as we sat together sharing a simple lunch at the table in the dining room of my house.

As the time neared for me to return to school following the break for lunch, Carl Erskine endorsed a photo and gave it to me as a memento of our meeting. On the reverse side of the photo he wrote: "To Patrick, Good Luck and Best Wishes, Your Friend, Carl Erskine."

Since that memorable day, I have kept carefully and securely the photo card given to me by Carl Erskine. He continued pitching for the Dodgers for a few more seasons until his retirement and his return to a life in Anderson. During his career, he pitched two no-hitters and claimed for many years the World Series single game strikeout record which he had compiled against the New York Yankees.

At the time of this writing, Carl Erskine is alive at age 93 and continues to reside in Anderson, Indiana. In the world of baseball, he is revered and praised for his humility, compassion, and respectful treatment of his loyal fans. Carl Erskine has authored two books about the Dodgers, and he sent me copies for my children, autographed with the inscription that matches the exact words he wrote for me in January, 1957.

Carl Erskine was a perfect hero and idol for a young boy in the 1950s in America. I still sense an emotional reaction within my body every time I remember that day and the genuine kindness he displayed in my house on Jay Street.

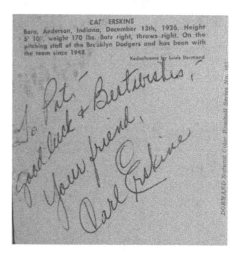

Message to Graduates

Here's a message to share with this year's graduates. It explains how to achieve success in being whomever you choose to be and doing whatever you choose to do during the remainder of your life on earth.

This is the secret. Do not tell a lie. That's the powerful formula for success. Five simple words contained in one simple sentence.

Follow that advice and most importantly the most important person in your life, that being you alone, will view yourself as a success despite whatever events are occurring around you in your life.

Never tell a lie to achieve a goal, however worthy that goal may seem to you at the moment you are tempted to tell a lie. Worthy goals should be limited by you to those accomplishments that can be attained by you without a need to tell a lie. If you have to tell a lie to achieve a goal it is a goal unworthy of you.

Do not tell a lie to your spouse, your parents, your siblings, your children, your relatives, your neighbors, your friends, your co-workers, your acquaintances, your adversaries, or strangers you may encounter on a single occasion in your life.

Lies erode your conscience and destroy your integrity, your self-esteem, and your sense of confidence.

Do not tell a lie to yourself. Never, ever lie to yourself about anything or anyone.

Be confident always that what you speak internally to yourself is only that which you believe to be truthful, and that you never will allow yourself to be fooled by the temptation of self-deception for any reason or for any purpose or under any circumstances whatsoever.

You likely will never win a lottery, you will never be president of any organization or country, you will not be canonized as a saint, you will not perform miracles, and you will not be the wealthiest person on earth, ever.

More likely, you will struggle financially because the bills always seem to surmount and exceed the balance in your checking account.

You, however, can and you will manage every crisis, every challenge, every obstacle you encounter during your life but only if and because you know the secret to success in life.

Simply, you will not tell a lie.

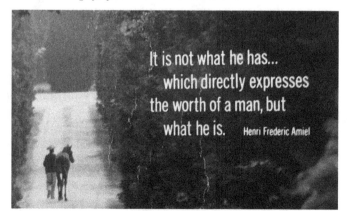

It is not what he has...
which directly expresses
the worth of a man, but
what he is. Henri Frederic Amiel

Who Were You, Davie Haynes?

Moving at a leisurely pace on a late afternoon stroll, walking along the south side of Seeley Street, just east of Morse Street, my attention froze on a gravesite in the far northeast corner of our community's most historical cemetery.

Why was this particular gravesite covered with heavy growth while the remainder of the cemetery lawn had been recently mowed? Why did it, alone, have a thick covering of foliage consisting of either bright green weeds or flowers awaiting the awakening of a late spring bloom of colorful petals?

My curiosity aroused, I entered the cemetery gate, to investigate the occupier of this grave. His name was, or should it be said, is Davie Haynes. Proclaimed on his stone is the epithet "Davie Haynes died March 28, 1854, age 42 years."

Why is Davie's the only grave site in this modest inner city burial plot that remains uncut today? Is this a subtle, subliminal level message being conveyed, possibly the expression of a memorial to the man whose bodily remains are sealed below the ground I now stand upon? Is this a ceremonial growth of edible plants, a tribute perhaps to a person who was a farmer? Or, are these flowers growing in memory of a beloved man who cherished the beauty of his personal flower garden? Is this a spiteful patch of weeds?

Who were you, Davie Haynes? Do your descendants gather solemnly at this site on March 28 each year, to pause, to memorialize, to pay a respectful tribute by recalling the narrative of your life? What would you say to us about life today, our incredible technological developments, our amazing systems for communicating, our vehicles for speedy travel, our fascination with immediate results, our selfish impatience?

Speak to us and tell us whether the condition of your grave site is a tribute or an embarrassment to you. We should know more about that life you lived for 42 years, a pioneer upon this land we now call our home. You departed 166 years ago, but there remain these visible reminders of you, Davie, at your grave site, marked by a worn stone, bearing the faded yet visible inscription of your name.

Dreams of Glory

After I returned to school to begin my 7th grade year at St. Joan of Arc in the two story brick building at the southwest corner of East Harrison and South Jay Streets, I had my sights set on a trajectory that would climax in my senior year of high school by leading my Kokomo Wildcats to a state basketball championship.

The previous March the Wildcats, led by the legendary shooting of Jimmy Rayl, had lost in the Saturday night final by a lopsided score. It seemed unfair that Kokomo had played a very tough New Albany team in an earlier game on the same day and entered the championship final understandably fatigued and exhausted whereas the eventual state champion, Crispus Attucks, easily and effortlessly, had blasted its opponent in the afternoon session.

To upgrade the quality of my game, it became necessary to move from the basketball hoop located behind the garage at my home to the competition offered on the paved courts at the northeast corner of the Meridian School lot. This locale near the corner of East Harrison and South Bell Streets was basketball heaven for the near south east side of Kokomo: four full length asphalt paved courts, eight sturdy iron rims with chain nets, and freshly painted out of bounds lines running north and south from basket to basket.

The fiercest competition always took place on the easternmost court nearest South Bell Street. And, as a seventh grader, I was both grateful and flattered when I was selected for inclusion on an impromptu team for a game to be played by the best of the very best in the neighborhood.

That's when I was introduced to Chuck Woolley. A 1958 recent graduate of Kokomo High School, and seven years older than me, after a day of hard work in the world of adults, Chuck would arrive at the Meridian School courts in a car that was the envy of his peers: a two tone painted Chevy with sleek rear extension fins, fashionable bubble skirts over the thick white side walled rear tires, a soft fabric set of dice floating on a string tied to the interior rear view mirror, and a California style" rake" lowering the front end. Of course, Chuck's car also had the absolute loudest decibel breaking chrome muffler pack in the entire city.

Woolley is remembered by me as usually playing basketball wearing jeans, tapered to a tight drape, a loose fitting front button cotton fabric short sleeved shirt, both sleeves rolled twice, the right sleeve tuck used for the convenient placement of a pack of cigarettes, and his feet fitted with either a pair of penny loafers or out of place and unpolished black wingtip shoes.

Woolley was always a "captain" and selected "his players" for a game to be played on the fabled east end court. No one challenged, disputed, or questioned Woolley's status.

And, that is how I met Chuck Woolley. He selected me as the fifth and final player for his roster, and during the game he fed me the ball for an easy layup. He made me feel wanted, that I was part of his team and he reinforced my dream to be a future Kokomo Wildcat running onto the majestic court at Memorial Gymnasium on Apperson Way.

My basketball dream never materialized or became reality. After my eighth grade graduation, I advanced to the top level courts located in Foster Park and against elite city wide competition I recognized quickly the summer of 1961 that I was too slow, too short, and too everything to play varsity basketball at the high school level. But, throughout high school, I continued to visit the courts regularly at Meridian School and enjoyed the competitive but friendly games played with my neighborhood friends.

Workshop of The Devil?

Idleness is greatly underrated. We fail as a community to recognize the importance of people who do nothing with their time. Not someone who does nothing all the time but selectively some of the time.

It's not easy being a top notch performer of idleness. It means training your mind to shut down, completely, totally, without exception for any thought of any possible value, meaning, or purpose. Thoughts can be the seed that starts a person on his or her way to meaningful activity. Therefore, the presence of any type of thought must be banished from the idle mind.

Idleness is not some form of transcendental meditation, introspective reflection, or contemplative tranquility. Those confused states of mind can be meaningful, even productive, and occasionally they can generate nasty ideas that lead to self-worth, recognition of purpose, realistic goal setting, altruism or volunteerism, and occasionally, work.

Possibly, you recognize this message is selfishly for me. It follows an empty week of near perfect idleness, interrupted by that intrusive request to consider exchanging my pursuit of perfect idleness for the performance of tasks that remain on my exponentially expanding summer "to do" list. But, resistance to the motivation of others has become my new trademark for a summer of inactivity.

Enough of this thinking and writing about the importance of being perfectly idle. No one can achieve the highest level of doing nothing by doing something. So, if you do not object, it is time again to lose my focus and return again to my quest for absolute nothingness.

Feeding America

A beautiful sight available to us in Branch County is the view of a field recently planted with the seeds for this year's crop. A field freshly tilled and marked with the straight rows of recently planted crops reminds us that our nourishment and survival are dependent upon the bountiful annual harvest of nutrient rich vegetables to be removed from the soil in late autumn.

A person who can claim the title of farmer is a person to be envied by us who sit at desks feeding or entering data into a lifeless keyboard or stand aside a work bench assembling or machining components into a finished product we may never see with our eyes or hold in our hands.

Farming is a noble enterprise. We are proud to describe Branch County as an agricultural community. To prepare the soil, to plant the seeds, to nurture growth arising from the ground, and to harvest the bountiful mature crop are tasks which every human should have the opportunity to experience in life.

We humans are unique in our symbiotic relationship with planet earth. No other living creature enjoys the communion which farming alone provides to the human participant. Those who farm have a special experience of the circle of life, the rotation of the seasons, and the blueprint of God's creation.

Indeed, as a nation we celebrate our farming heritage in the timeless lyrics of a cherished song in which we proudly proclaim the beauty of our amber waves of grain, purple mountain majesties, above the fruited plains.

There is no occupation in America more American than the job of a farmer. God truly shed his grace on thee.

A Special Friend

He was on the eve of celebrating his 99th birthday. Working that summer as an intern at a local newspaper, the assignment was passed to my desk to visit the Good Samaritan nursing home and interview George Hewitt.

What do you ask a person whose mind is sharp but whose body is weak on the day before his 99th birthday? You do not ask. You listen. As a young man 21 years old, there was much for me to hear and to learn in that brief interview with a person who had been born a few short years after Lee and Grant's historic meeting at the Appomattox Court House in 1865.

Dressed in a crisp white shirt, accented by a colorful bowtie, shoes radiating a sparkling buffed shine, sitting in his wheelchair in his modestly decorated nursing home room, George Hewitt invited me into his world that summer day. For two hours we visited, my listening, his talking, words shared by him with me about his fascinating and adventurous life.

George Hewitt went on to live another four years until his death at the age of 103 years in June, 1972. Many times, during vacations from college and law school, and while home for summer break, it was a treat for me to visit with him.

We became friends. He had no living descendants. He began to regard me as his family. Towards the end of his life, he would not let go of this earth until my graduation from law school, my promised return to his dying bedside, fulfillment of my pledge to deliver to him my diploma for his eyes to see and his hands to touch. Two weeks later, he was gone from us.

We should give prayerful thanks for the lives of those whose words, kindness, support, laughter, and smiles have enriched our experience of human life. There is a George Hewitt present or waiting to be discovered in every life, whose hand needs to be touched softly, whose shoulders await an embrace, whose life should be celebrated as if it was his 99th birthday.

Acrobatic Flyers: Rollers

During my late adolescent pre-teen years every boy living in my near south east side neighborhood who interacted with me on a frequent basis raised pigeons. We had our separate pigeon coops built in our backyards and we alone were responsible for feeding our birds daily, and keeping their water bowl filled with water for drinking and bathing, both of which are crucial activities for pigeons.

All of the pigeons in our neighborhood could trace their ancestry to pigeons owned and raised by a man who lived at the very end of South Cooper Street, named Roland Fain. He was a kind man who always welcomed us when we rode our bikes to his house, knocked on his back door, and asked him if it was okay for us to open and enter the "gated community" which housed the buildings occupied by a menagerie of birds, guinea pigs, and chickens. Roland trusted us and always gave his permission for us to enter and look around at the animals he maintained in that large pen he had built in his backyard.

Roland was a friend to young boys when mature men could be friends to young boys without raising concerns about improper intentions. He never behaved or spoke to us in any inappropriate or manipulative manner. He, simply, enjoyed raising and maintaining his collection of pigeons, guinea pigs, and chickens and was flattered by the interest we had in his hobby.

We boys purchased our pigeons from Roland's flock of birds, and placed them in the pens each of us had built in the backyard at our respective houses. My flock began with the purchase of a cock and hen, Big Tom and Dismasrelda, who mated and produced nests of baby pigeons called squabs, all of which were sold or given away by me, with the exception of a bird I kept and named Cleopatra.

My pigeons would be released from their pen daily, allowing them to take flight, exercise, and eventually return to the pen by sunset. The breed of pigeons we owned was called "rollers," and given that name in recognition of their acrobatic flying style; the breed would pause during flight, perform a magical series of backward somersaults while descending towards but not to the surface of the ground, and then abruptly redirect their trajectory upwards flying high into the sky. They would repeat this remarkable maneuver each time they spread their wings and flew away from a stationery perch.

Rollers also are very beautiful pigeons. They have colorful feathers, and stripes arranged in a variety of neat linear patterns. They would eat feed grain held in the palm of my hand, and if coaxed would perch on my extended index finger.

I raised pigeons for about three years and lost interest in them as I advanced through high school. By the time I left home to attend college, I had found a new home for my pigeons and disassembled the wooden framed and wire fenced coop which had been built adjacent to the south side of the detached garage at my house.

Take It All In

My seven month old grandson achieved a milestone in his young life last week.

Reportedly, he managed to raise himself upwards with his arms and stood on the mattress alongside the railings of his crib.

Good for Brendan. He was simply responding to the inherited DNA triggered instinct that the world becomes significantly more interesting when its features are viewed in an upright position.

Everything seems out of focus when observed flat on your back looking straight upwards, or from the wobbly vantage point created by the experience of being held in the tight embrace of another person's arms.

We welcome Brendan to our view of the world we inhabit here on our planet Earth.

However, he eventually will be confronted by his need to find his means to maintain throughout his life the infant's sense of fascination with objects around us, that wonderful perpetual urge for moments of pure discovery, that passion to encounter and to connect with the shared humanity concealed behind those faces seen by his eyes.

We share the path of all pilgrims walking in search of an encounter with the instructive flow of energy generated by the fuel of our basic human instincts, seeking the sensation of that creative urge which invites us to rise up on the stage of life and stand independently on our feet, yearning for that moment when our eyes look outward and we experience in this unique moment of time the remarkable natural beauty of the world in which we live.

When we stand and view the world as Brendan did when he stood for the first time in his crib, we share with him that moment of joyful discovery.

We, too, recognize in the reality of our lives sufficient evidence to support our shared proclamation of faith that our life today on earth is only the childhood of our everlasting immortality.

Just Being There

Being both a son and a father, a few words from me about Father's Day seem appropriate this week. Everyone has a father. He may be your biological father, your adopted father, your stepfather, your foster father, or your relative or family friend who doubles as your father. He is your Dad, regardless.

What's most important is the presence of a male figure in your life, someone who provides an example to you about style, about attitude, and about family. From whomever you obtain those life lessons, that person should be regarded as your Dad.

Being a father means a relationship that transcends mere biological connections. It is a relationship built upon a foundation of loving, caring, nurturing, supporting, and respecting the individuality of both father and child.

A father does not live through the accomplishments of his child. He celebrates those achievements but he does not claim them as his moments of glory. A father applauds the uniqueness of his child's talents and encourages his son or daughter to be the person he or she is capable of being on this planetary home we call earth.

Take a look around in your family or community and you will identify that person who needs the nourishment of a father. Then do something about it. You will discover that the relationship will provide you with some of the most memorable moments of your life.

Alone Together

The Pennsylvania Railroad tracks crossing East Vaile Avenue in a north/south direction near and east of South Locke Street and west of the red brick Cuneo Press main factory building were a daily source of visual fascination for me and my adolescent age friends residing in the modest houses inside the near south east side neighborhoods of Kokomo, during the mid and late 1950s.

The tracks were bustling with the roar of rail traffic during those years. The terminal was located a few blocks north of downtown Kokomo, alongside Main Street. Passengers were being transported to disembark at the local train station or to remain onboard and continue traveling northwest towards Chicago.

Standing on the north side of East Vaile Avenue, within thirty yards of the tracks, we could see brief, momentary glimpses of the faces of the passengers seated inside the train. Their upper bodies and faces were most sharply defined near dawn or dusk, early morning or late evening, when the inside of the railroad car was illuminated by artificial lighting used to accommodate the convenience of the onboard passengers.

The passengers on the train appeared to be a variety of ages, from toddlers to elders, traveling to either a near or faraway destination that would provide either cherished lasting memories of a special trip taken or very faint, if any, memory of a trip whose descriptive details were forgotten many years ago.

I never recognized the face of a traveler seated at the window inside the passenger car on the train, whose curious eyes were staring back, seeing me and my friends as a group of unidentified and anonymous boys standing rigid while attentively observing the movement of a passing train.

Within a minute, it was over, the fleeting experience had passed, and my friends and I would return to whatever activity we had been doing before we paused to view the windows of the passing train and to glance at the passengers sitting inside.

I never encountered in any situation in my future a person who would be identified by me as a passenger who had been aboard a train watched by me as its tracks crossed East Vaile Avenue advancing towards or away from the trestle that enabled the train to travel across the streaming water of the Wildcat Creek, whose rippling current flowed from east to west as it progressed through Kokomo.

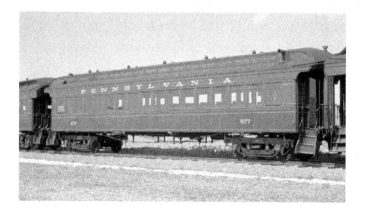

That you and I are living on an orbiting planet occupied not only by you and me but also shared with a near infinite number of other living creatures or things whose physical bodies have defining features that resemble the shape and structure of you and me is a miracle.

Should you and I be living on an orbiting planet occupied by you or me, alone, void and absent the presence of any living creatures or things whose physical bodies have defining features that resemble the shape and structure of you and me would be a tragedy.

I saw you passing by me as you traveled as a passenger on the train riding to wherever your destination was to be on that day when you briefly saw me and I briefly saw you, and we both recognized in our mutual shared minute of anonymity that human life is not a sad tragedy but rather a wonderful miracle of possibility. Pilgrims on a journey, we are.

In that passing moment, we knew that life is its own excuse for being.

Add Extra Onions and Chili Sauce

Maybe you missed it last week. But, certainly by now you are aware of it. Allen's Root Beer Stand on West Chicago Street has reopened for the season. Put away the firewood, woolen gloves, fur hats, hot chocolate mix and welcome the arrival of spring.

Hopefully, no one in our home county is so uninformed that he or she misses the significance of that memorable event. It defines the calendar, the changing of the seasons, the welcoming of blissful spring breezes, the slow but certain approach of summer fun, dips in the pool to escape drenching humidity, and the unique refreshment of root beer served up generously to us in a traditional frost covered glass mug.

While change surrounds us, some important things about our lives are not meant or allowed to change. A root beer stand is one of those things.

Girls still tend to the cars that pull into the carefully painted and perfectly aligned parking spots, made to order food and drink are delivered on a tray affixed to your lowered window, and when you finish, simply turn on your headlights to signal for prompt clean up service.

Since attachment of the Allen family's trademark name to the preparation of that first order for a coney island hot dog topped off with an abundance of delicious chopped onions and a generous portion of meat sauce, aside a sack of hot, fresh and tasteful French fries, together with an ice cold root beer, was delivered to a customer's car window many years ago, we locals have learned to recognize the most accurate and reliable signal of spring's annual arrival --- our community root beer stand, open for business again.

Searching For Emma

In the past week a significant amount of my time has been used to search the internet for information about my ancestral roots. Genealogical research has an addictive quality that can grasp you in its grip. There is some form of euphoric or climactic burst of exuberance that accompanies a breakthrough moment when you finally solve the puzzle and identify the names of Grandma Emma's parents.

However, I am still searching tirelessly for the hidden identity of my great grandmother's parents. I desperately want to identify her parents to allow me to proceed backwards in time to confirm the oral history given to me that there is flowing in my arteries and veins the rich blood of a Native American Cherokee.

I have labored my way back through the labyrinth of my roots to the early seventeenth century. I have discovered the presence of a father and son who fought on separate sides in the Civil War, an ancestor who in his first months of infancy sailed aboard a flimsy ship in the early 18th century crossing the Atlantic Ocean, leaving Europe with his parents for the opportunity of a new world in America.

I proudly discovered ancestors who fought alongside other patriots in the Connecticut militia during the Revolutionary War.

All of us have ancestors. Some were good, some not so good. The fact is, however, that we would not be here today unless our ancestors had lived the lives they lived, providing a necessary link in the human chromosome chain that allows our nomadic and eternal spirits to appear in bodily form in the time and place we call now.

Obviously, there is no means by which we can directly thank our ancestors for the hardships they endured, the pain they withstood, the obstacles they overcame, the faith they embraced, without which I would not be here to write and speak and you would not be here to read and listen to these words today.

I am going to continue the search for the identity of Emma's parents. She managed to survive the deaths of two infant children, a difficult trip in a horse drawn wagon migrating to the Yankee states from the Smokey Mountains of east Tennessee, and daily life with a Victorian Era chauvinistic Scotch Irish husband. I owe it to Grandma Emma to identify for my future descendants that Cherokee chief reportedly in her ancestral tree.

Celebrate Winter?

Now that November has arrived, it is time to begin planning for the winter season. There is absolutely no reason to deny the fact that before you know it or can say the words "winter blizzard," the holiday season will be a memory only, and the dark days of winter will be the story of our lives.

There must be something good about winter, the shortened daylight hours, the ice on my windshield, the salty slush on my shoes, the hacking cough, scratchy throat and stuffy nose, the slippery walks and perilous roads. When you discover what is good about the cruel days of winter, please alert me to the revelation of your surprise discovery.

On second thought, we do have mugs of hot chocolate, midnight walks through a freshly fallen snow, views of the brightest stars of the year sprinkled across a natural canvas of pitch black skies, the glow of the embers sizzling in the pit of a brick fireplace, and the occasional perfectly timed snow day.

Nothing happens in the summer to match the exhilaration of a snow day in the middle of a lousy winter. It's Mother Nature's gift to all, a free card allowing us to stay home, sleep late, read a great book, take a midday nap, and dream contentedly about the horrific misery of suffocating blast furnace skin scorching humidity produced by a blazing sun in July.

As Forrest Gump advised us, life is like a box of chocolates. Not every piece you select will be what you had hoped to pull from the box. Learn to live and enjoy what you have in your hand, whether it is a butter cream, a chocolate mint, a peanut cluster, a sweet cherry filled middle, or a chewy caramel.

Every day is just a piece of candy.

Seasonal Changes

Winter does have its better moments, those times when we gaze into the light of the street lamps and become entranced by the dance of the white crystal snowflakes cascading through the air, a majestic cardinal perched on a leafless branch in a front yard tree, a deer wandering in search of food through a woods adjacent to a farmhouse, children sledding on a hill or ice skating on a pond.

We yearn for the season of spring. I want to ride my bike around the city in the evening, to see people sitting on their front porch steps or enjoying from a park bench the view of ducks swimming in the creek. I want to see colorful blooms on early spring flowers, grass sprouting a fresh coat of green, and people populating the sidewalks on an evening stroll through town.

We lust for summer with its sizzling sand on a beach, the refreshment of a jump into an inviting backyard pool, a movie under the stars at a drive-in theatre, an ice cold frosty mug filled to the rim with root beer brought on the tray attached to my car window at a local root beer stand, long days brought to a spectacular close by a brilliant sunset painted onto the western horizon of the sky.

The fall season is terrific, too. The fabulous blending of colors sprinkled onto the leaves of trees, the special scent in the autumn air, the annual return to school, pumpkins to carve and cold cider to drink, the hint of anticipation as we recognize the approach of a future Thanksgiving and a festive Christmas ahead.

There are plenty of reasons to like whatever season it is in which we happen to live at any moment in our life. It's variety, it's change, it's who we are, it's life, and if we had a choice, we would not have it any other way.

Gripe, Gripe, and More Gripes

It is that time of the year when it would seem appropriate to express, vent, and complain about everything in daily life that causes aggravation for me. It is clear that my personality has balance, my life virtue, and my mind a firm grip on reality, traits qualifying me for the right to let it rip and speak my mind.

Gripe number one is the person who insists on talking on his or her cell phone while driving on the road. It is not simply the act of talking on the phone but it is the way it appears to be done by the offending driver. You can see the person's lips moving, head bobbing, eyes glazing, as the distracted driver turns in front of my car, or claims a right of way that exists in my favor.

Gripe number two also concerns use of a cell phone. This complaint is about the nitwit who insists on using the highest volume possible while talking on a cell phone in a restaurant. This habit not only allows but mandates that every other person in the restaurant has to share in one side only of the private conversation being broadcast to every booth, chair, and table in the restaurant.

Gripe number three is the person driving in front of me who makes a right turn into a parking lot aside a busy commercial street, and with the rear half of the vehicle protruding onto the road, this bozo stops to view the landscape of parked cars already in the lot. This is a rear end collision difficult to avoid.

Gripe number four is the Good Samaritan who stops on the roadway, to wave another driver to proceed and cross in front, without the person doing the waving having any idea as to what might be approaching from the rear in the next lane. Just swallow the temptation to do a good deed and do not wave a person to drive across in front of your vehicle unless you have eyes in the back of your head to allow you to see whether there is another vehicle moving up on the rear of your vehicle in an adjoining lane to your left or right.

Gripe number five is anyone who is so stupid as to disagree with anything said or written by me. One thing clear to me about life is that it is clear to me that everything but me seems rather messed up. So do not tell me that what is said by me is something that is wrong, erroneous, or otherwise should not have been said.

It is so hot. When will winter return?

Captain Midnight

My favorite winter season beverage is a mug of hearty and robust Ovaltine. It is advertised, as least it was in the 1950s, as being fortified and enriched with vitamins and minerals essential for a young boy's growth.

However, I am no longer a young boy according to the national census and I am no longer growing in height but only expanding in measurement of the circumference of my girth.

My introduction to hot Ovaltine (never drink it cold) came via the Saturday morning television series named Captain Midnight. In each adventurous episode he was a daring, jut jawed war hero who led a mysterious government group called the Secret Squadron. The show began in late 1954 and concluded in early 1957, after only 39 original episodes broadcast on the CBS network. For me, that brief span covered the impressionable ages of seven to nine years old.

I was all in, totally loyal and absolutely devoted to assisting in the mission of the week with Captain Midnight. Usually, I would sit in front of our laminated plywood cabinet that encased our black and white television set, wearing my Captain Midnight pajamas. Two added items were essential to be properly uniformed: the special decoder ring and my member's name and serial number identification card.

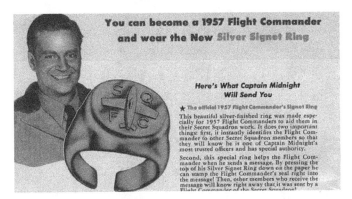

At the end of each episode, a clue was given for members of the youth squadron to solve by use of the revolving piece mounted on top of the decoder ring. The answer would be revealed and utilized in the next episode to assist Captain Midnight in the completion of his always very dangerous mission which had its usual climactic conclusion featuring his timely rescue of a frightened damsel in distress.

At the end of each episode, I would move to the kitchen and my Mom would prepare hot Ovaltine for me to drink from my very special and authentic deep red Captain Midnight plastic mug. I still have it but I no longer use it to drink hot Ovaltine, fearing that the aged plastic exposed to a hot beverage would melt or poison me or both. I do, however, treasure that mug, although it has only sentimental and not a collector's value to me.

Often, the best shows on television are discontinued too soon. That happens today and it certainly happened to Captain Midnight on the CBS network in late January, 1957.

Of course, being able to adjust and carry on in the face of disappointment and adversity is the courageous behavior Captain Midnight would expect from a registered member of his youth squadron, a person like me. Maybe it is time to take a risk in my life and again pour a steaming hot portion of rich chocolate flavored Ovaltine into my historic red plastic Captain Midnight mug.

Life So Joyful!

Is there any time in life filled with more expectation than the arrival of the first week of April?

It signals life triumphant, the dawn of a new beginning, a rebirth, the arousal of nature from its winter slumber, the shedding of dark hues replaced soon by brilliant and majestic color schemes decorating the earth with a prism of light, its radiance spreading across the landscape.

How could a person believe that life is the product of a Darwinian process of natural selection, only? To examine with a microscope the petals of a flower, to witness a bird in flight, to gaze upon the stars in the sky at night, those simple moments in life attest to the fact that this mystery we call life is not the result of an accidental occurrence, but the creation of a wondrous loving spirit whom we most reverently refer to as the Creator.

The passing of a season and the arrival of a new reminds us that we are participants in the circle of life.

My favorite day of spring is that first day of exceptionally warm weather when the parks fill in the evening with the joyful shouts of children romping on the slides and swings in the playground, youthful athletes choosing sides for a game on the soccer field, the baseball diamond, or basketball and tennis courts, cars again parking along the shoulder of the winding narrow road near the bank of the creek flowing serenely through the city park.

Life is a mystery to be lived, not a problem to be solved.

It Is I You Send

For those who are suffering with a troubled marriage, a delinquent child, a quarrelsome but unavoidable relative, an insecure job position, or insufficient money to pay for the most basic monthly necessities, Christmas season can be a time that seems to enhance the emotional pain.

Life is a mixture of good and bad, bitter and the sweet, achievements and disappointments, joy and sorrow.

We have the capacity to share our time with other humans. We pilgrims do not make this earth journey alone. We are castaways in a boat whose frightened occupants can give to each other hope, encouragement, and love.

My favorite song of contemporary Christian music is titled "Here I Am Lord." The refrain seeks an answer from God: Is it I you call? I have heard you calling in the night. Whom shall you send?

The singer asks if it is he who is called to bear God's light, to hold others in his heart, to tend to the poor and lame, to be an instrument of peace, to feed the hungry among us the finest bread.

In the final analysis, human life is a present tense experience the worth of which is measured not by our collection of possessions or accumulation of wealth but by our empathy for and response to the suffering, the loneliness, the relentless pain, and the desperation of others. Quietly and patiently listen; be accessible, forgiving, understanding, but be not judgmental.

During this holy advent season, that pleading voice you hear is the Holy Spirit, calling to you, sending you to be a messenger of God's love. Yes, it is I you send, Lord.

Beyond Our Control

Sometimes the wind believes that it can control our lives. It has the physical strength to direct, restrict, and limit our activities. Its ferocity can force us to seek shelter inside a dwelling.

Accompanying sheets of rain, a surge of wind can force us to lower an umbrella and surrender to the involuntary soaking of our clothes. Walking against the wind, leaning forward, trapped in the sensation of standing directly behind the wind blast produced by the blades of a turbine engine, we lose our balance, stumble, waiver, wobble, unable to navigate forward movement in a straight line.

Conversely, there are days of extreme humidity when a cool breeze passing across the damp skin of our perspiring forehead brings us comfort, refreshment, a momentary escape from the imprisonment of near suffocating and sweltering midsummer heat.

We open our arms and embrace that frigid cool flow of wind circulating from the vents on our air conditioners, allowing us to function productively, work, recreate, relax, in an indoors environment without hearing the sizzle of our brains being fried by stifling heat and humidity.

That eternal spirit from whom all life arises, the source of that essential flow of electricity, the provider of our connection to the transmission of energy that is required for the existence of human life, selects from an assortment of natural tools such as the wind, to remind us of the arrogance of our faith, the foolishness of our vanity, our dependence upon forces beyond our control, and our perpetual need to engage in humble prayer by which we seek and petition for the gifts of humility, charity, and inspiration.

The wind reminds us of a message we should never forget living each day under the spell of the delusions of power and control.

My Land in the Wilderness

At the mature old age of eight years, in 1955, I decided to become a careful land speculator. My first parcel of real estate consisted of one square inch of vacant land located, supposedly, in the Yukon Territory in the far northwest region of Canada.

I have a piece of paper which is a deed evidencing my title or ownership to my property in the Yukon wilderness. And, I am an attorney so I am prepared now to defend my rights and privileges of ownership all the way to the Supreme Court, if necessary. Believe it, please, that you do not want to mess with me in court.

I found this rare opportunity for land ownership during my days as a devoted fan of the Sergeant Preston of the Yukon television series, which also featured his loyal husky wonder dog, King. I never missed viewing a weekly episode on our first generation purchased on sale at Wards black and white family television set.

The sponsor of the series was the Quaker Oats Company, more specifically, its cereal brand known as Puffed Rice. (Truthfully, I preferred the Puffed Oats but I ate the Puffed Rice daily in deference to Sergeant Preston's sincere endorsement of the bowl of nutritious breakfast rice over oats.)

Some brilliant advertising executive in the marketing department decided to launch a promotion which would lure and encourage kids to hassle mom to buy the Sergeant Preston's favorite breakfast cereal brand because only found inside that secure box would be the coupon to be completed and returned to the manufacturer in exchange for a valuable deed to one square inch of vacant land somewhere in the remote Yukon Territory.

Amazingly, there really was vacant land situated in the pristine Yukon forest purchased by the cereal maker to legitimatize its generous giveaway promotion. A survey was made to create parcel descriptions for a vacant plot consisting of a total of 19.1 acres thereafter to be subdivided into millions of one square inch tracts.

A local attorney in the Yukon Territory, who likely had a scarcity of fee paying corporate clients, was hired to confirm and he, in fact, did so affirm by sworn affidavit that the property deeds would be legal without any requirement for filing of each with the register of deeds.

If you are interested in arranging for legal services to be provided in the Yukon Territory, the attorney's name is George Van Roggen. However, it is likely that George is either retired or no longer alive and living among us.

My individual parcel is reportedly located near the village of Whitehorse, approximately seven miles up the Yukon River.

I have never visited the wild and remote Yukon Territory to examine my property to evaluate its usefulness as a future homestead. Maybe a tiny house would fit my needs.

I am giving serious thought to making a trip now that I am not aging any younger by the year but only becoming older and less mobile. Also, my wife is encouraging me to go ahead, be bold and adventurous, and make a wilderness trip to claim physical possession of my land situated in the desolate forests of the Yukon Territory.

There is a problem, however.

Reportedly, for non-payment of taxes my property and millions of other one inch square parcels divided up by Quaker Oats and conveyed by deed to me and others included in the now elder population count of my accomplished baby boom generation were sold and purchased at a tax sale by the regional government for a price of $37.20 at auction in 1965. No fair!

That has to be a violation of due process. And, that's where my being an attorney will be the spear that pierces the medieval armored shield of the Canadian government.

So, here's the deal. If you have one of the deeds for a parcel in the Yukon Territory that you received from the Quaker Oats Company around 1955, send me your name, address, and phone number with a certified check or redeemable for cash or merchandise Costco's gift card in the amount of $150.00 and, be assured, that I will faithfully represent your legal interests!

Wait! There's more! When I visit the Yukon Territory I will take a photo of your property and transmit it by email to you for an added $25.00 necessary only to cover my travel costs.

This is a deal that you cannot afford to pass up. Particularly today, real estate can be the only can't miss or no way to fail investment tool. Believe me. I know what I am talking about. I am a really good lawyer.

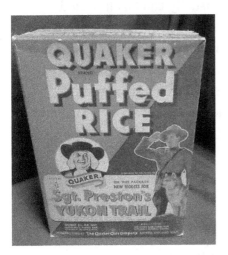 

Finding Excuses

Is it enjoyable to rake leaves? My spouse has been trying to convince me of that belief for many years.

First, way too many sacrifices are required of a man to embrace with enthusiasm the activity of raking leaves. Foremost, is the interference it poses in terms of reducing significantly the time spent on a couch watching a weekend's menu of college and professional football. Live television means watching each game simultaneous with its occurrence although a convenient remote is required for multiple game viewing.

Also, the exercise required for the movement of raking guarantees a morning after of regrets. You can expect a sore back, tired shoulders, blistered hands, and painful forearm muscles. By comparison, my body never aches after a weekend of watching football on television, although occasionally there is a twinge in the wrists consistent with the symptoms of carpal tunnel syndrome.

The problems with the wrists usually can be alleviated promptly by proper rest, namely a late afternoon or early evening dual Saturday and Sunday naps on the couch. A good weekend nap is greatly misunderstood by my spouse and most women similarly situated in life, being married to a man who seems to lack the motivation necessary to pick up a rake and use it vigorously on the weekends.

Besides, leaves should be left alone on the lawn. It is my fervent belief, without being influenced by any thoughts of selfish preferences, that allowing the leaves to remain on the lawn literally guarantees they will become the neighbor's problem after they are swept away from my yard by the last gale winds of the autumn. Why rake the leaves when you can leave the task for someone else to do?

As you can readily see, there are many valid reasons for my opposition to my wife's perennial honey do list for autumn weekends, always highlighted at the top of her ten point list by the inclusion of leave raking for my weekend activities. Sometimes reason must prevail over emotions. It seems very reasonable to me to spend my weekends with a couch, a remote, my television, a nap, and of course, a supply of tasty but unhealthy snacks.

That reminds me. Someone needs to make a trip to the grocery and restock the pantry shelves with some chips, mixed nuts, and fresh chocolate chip cookies before next weekend.

Are you too busy right now or can you help me?

Land of Guns

My Dad and I would occasionally hunt for rabbits from early November to the end of the Christmas and New Year's holiday season. I had no interest in hunting deer or other animals.

I began hunting rabbits with my Dad when he purchased for me a new single shot Beretta model rifle when I reached the age of 13 years in 1960. From that time forward, he would hunt only with me because he trusted my respect for gun safety and he felt secure walking through a recently harvested farm field or in woodlands accompanied by me. Likewise, I had absolute trust and confidence in his adherence to the rules of safe hunting.

My present memory is that we usually went hunting when the ground was covered with fresh snow, ideal conditions for following rabbit tracks. There was a sense of refreshment being outdoors in bitterly cold, frigid air participating in an ancient primordial father and son experience with my Dad.

Actually, we were never very successful in our hunt for rabbits. If we did manage occasionally to shoot a rabbit, my Dad would clean and dress it in the woods, wrap it in a plastic bag, and bring it home with us to serve as the main dish in a supper later in the week. What we shot we kept and we ate, respectful of the hunter's creed to avoid shooting animals only for the purpose of mere amusement.

After my law school years, I moved away from home and my Dad and I never again hunted for rabbits. Indeed, he put our rifles away in a safe storage location and never again used his rifle for any purpose. He and I did keep our memories of the hunting experiences we shared together.

My Dad's rifle and my rifle have been passed on to the ownership of my younger son who has a high level of respect for safe use of firearms. He is an outdoorsman type of man who enjoys hunting, fishing, target shooting, and archery. He finds no enjoyment in the use of firearms for the meaningless shooting of animals.

Ownership of firearms is soaked into the fabric of America unlike any other society on our planet. Application of the Second Amendment "right to bear arms" has been stretched beyond the limits of any reasonable interpretation of its original intent. Its words create a tension in our country's politics that seems to evade a practical solution. Illegal use of guns has cast a deadly plague upon our land.

Saluting Katie the Teacher

Last week was national Teacher Appreciation Week throughout America. But, teachers should be appreciated every week, not only during a single designated week each year. Except for fighting fires, approaching a suspicious car on the side of the road, or fighting our battles overseas, there is no tougher job than the job of a teacher.

It is difficult to maintain discipline, attentiveness, and an environment conducive to learning in a classroom populated by a platoon of judgmental youngsters, adolescents, or teenagers. You better be good at the task or the task will eat you for lunch, each day of the week.

My favorite teacher is a person I never had as a teacher in the classroom. She is Katie, my daughter, who inspires me everyday with her dedication to the teaching profession. After completing her undergraduate education at Notre Dame in 2002, Katie launched her teaching career as a volunteer in Teach for America. In a setting lacking friends or family, she devoted her life to teaching students in an overpopulated classroom in an impoverished border town along the Rio Grande River in Texas.

After Texas, Katie relocated to the near south side of Chicago, where she labored daily in ghetto schools, teaching anxious children hungry for knowledge but hampered by the disadvantages of extreme poverty, drug infested neighborhoods, and absent or disconnected parents.

Today, Katie reports to work each morning to a sparkling classroom of middle school students where she inspires young minds to share her love of reading, writing, and speaking. She is a rare gem that sparkles. Parents appreciate her special talents and her students treasure her guidance.

National appreciation day is a worthy idea that deserves our support. Better yet would be a community that remembers each day of the week the contributions teachers make to the quality of life around us. It's a lesson we should have learned by now: say thank you, every day, to a teacher.

My Friend, Nipper

Every child should have a pet, preferably a dog. My childhood pet was a golden haired cocker spaniel named Nipper.

Nipper was added to our family when she was a pup and I was four years old. She died in 1966, after living with us for 15 years; I was away at college, in my first year at Notre Dame, when my Mom informed me that Nipper had been taken by my Dad to the vet to be euthanized due to the totally debilitating effects of a massive stroke she had suffered a few days before.

Nipper was my constant companion. We were truly inseparable. Wherever I went, Nipper went with me. If I watched a movie at a theatre located in downtown Kokomo, Nipper would wait outside for me to exit and to return at the end of the movie. When I walked to and from school in my elementary school years, she walked with me the one block distance from my house to St. Joan of Arc at the corner of Jay and Harrison Streets. Nipper would wait outside the school building, disregarding weather conditions, until the students dispersed at the end of each school day.

For the first five or six years of her life, Nipper would sleep outside in a dog house my Dad had built for her, placed on the south side of the detached garage located behind our house. In the coldest months of winter, we would place a small rug inside the dog house to add warmth for her. Eventually, my Dad's heart grew soft and he relented, giving his permission for Nipper to sleep inside our house, on a small platform at the bottom of the three steps up from the ground to the main floor.

Nipper could see with only her right eye. With a friend, I had been playing catch with a baseball, and it was thrown into the branches of a leafy tree; Nipper glanced up to investigate the sound in the tree above her, and suddenly the ball fell onto her left eye, shattering her cornea. She never carried a grudge or blamed any person for the unfortunate accident that caused her to lose all vision in her left eye.

Indeed, Nipper never blamed or accused any person of any slight or injury she experienced during her life. She was forgiving as a good dog is forgiving of our trespasses against her. She asked us only for simple acts of kindness in exchange for her unconditional loyalty. She never gossiped or criticized others.

Nipper taught me many important lessons about relationships. She seemed to like being with me for no particular reason except that she wanted and valued my companionship. Just my being me was enough for Nipper. Real friends display that pure form of absolute acceptance.

Be Honest and Truthful

A few days ago, my grandson, Patrick Benedict Rocchio, age five, played his first game of miniature golf alone with me. It was a teaching opportunity for me and a learning experience for him.

Too often we hurry to begin a challenging task without having made the proper adjustments and necessary preparations to maximize our opportunity to achieve our goals.

Clarifying a goal is important and without that clarity a person never really knows when the activity results in fulfillment of its purpose. A goal not only must be challenging and require focus to achieve but also it must be capable of being accomplished. Our goal was to use the golf club to hit the ball into the hole and to count each and every stroke taken in playing the game.

There must be no cheating in playing the game by its stated rules. Failing to include on the scorecard the actual number of strokes taken is an act of cowardice. Cheating is an expression of corrosive self-doubt. People who succeed do not believe it is necessary to cheat to be a winner.

To succeed at miniature golf a person must focus on the task of hitting the ball into the hole. Each stroke of the ball with the club must be performed without any distraction by the result of the prior stroke or anticipation of the next stroke. Live each present moment without either regret for the past or anxiety for the future.

After playing eighteen holes, my grandson returned his golf ball and club to the cashier and we departed in my car. It was a special time for the youthful pupil and his seasoned teacher, sharing not only the joyful experience of togetherness but also a lesson in the universal rules of life.

My Universe of 5 (x) 3 Square Blocks

The location of my birth and the community in which I lived the first 18 years of my life is named Kokomo. Labeled by its self-promoters as the "City of Firsts," Kokomo is situated at the midpoint of northcentral Indiana, designated as the county seat of Howard County.

In the year of my birth, 1947, my family's home was located at 701 South Jay Street, in a house my Dad had built with the help of a carpenter friend in anticipation of his marriage to my Mom, to occur in November, 1939. The simple family unit consisted of my parents, Benedetto (Benny) and Beulah; my older sister, Janice, born in 1942; and, of course, me, named Patrick Kent Rocchio.

Kokomo's population during the years of 1947 through 1965 averaged 40,000 inhabitants. Its economy was highly dependent upon middle class factory wages. The major employers were Delco Radio, Chrysler, Continental Steel, and Haynes Stellite; together, they employed 20,000 union laborers performing their services in exchange for a living wage.

My Mom was a housewife or to describe her career by use of a more modern moniker, she was a homemaker; during the years in which my sister and I resided at home, Mom's principal occupation or singular role was being "at the ready" to respond to any immediate need displayed by her children.

My Dad during his prime adult years was employed as a furnace operator in a foundry department at Haynes Stellite, later known simply as Stellite, after its purchase by Union Carbide. His daily assigned job was performed under less than ideal conditions; in other words, the work environment was hot, dirty, and often dangerous.

But, he did what he had to do while accumulating his record of perfect attendance because that devotion to work attendance was necessary to provide modest but essential financial security for his family.

The territorial universe of my childhood was defined by Vaile Avenue and the Wildcat Creek to the north, Waugh Street to the east, Markland Avenue to the south, and Apperson Way to the west, comprising a total surface area bordered by a distance of 5 blocks east and west and 3 blocks north and south.

Almost everything of any significance experienced prior to my mid-teen years occurred within those neighborhood boundaries.

There in the near south east side of Kokomo my closest friends resided, my newspaper route existed, my elementary school stood, and my influential church presided, each both separately and together contributing to the formation of the personal identity of who I was then and who I am today.

There are times when I do like myself. Thank you, Kokomo.

It Should Be So Simple

The two most powerful forces in human life are extending forgiveness and expressing an apology to others.

Too often people seem hesitant to acknowledge a mistake or a misdeed. Liability insurance companies and their lawyers instruct us never to admit fault for the harm our negligence may have caused another person. Is avoidance of responsibility or accountability for our actions and omissions, however, the best choice for us?

If someone injures us or causes us to lose property or other valuables, is it beneficial for us to seek revenge, to pursue the recovery of unjust compensation, or to inflict injury upon those who have trespassed against us?

Is our human nature so flawed that it is unrealistic to expect us to be capable of forgiving and apologizing? To forgive or to apologize makes us vulnerable, exposes us to risk, and could be considered as a display of submissive weakness. But, is that a valid perception upon which to base our actions?

All human achievement and accomplishment began somewhere and that somewhere is always the beginning. Each of us selects the conduct that will contain the definition of our uniqueness as a person.

It is the ultimate act of faith to grant forgiveness and to express an apology to others without any promise, guarantee or certainty that we will not be hurt or harmed by our kind behavior.

It is not easy either to forgive or to apologize. What is easy is not always what is best for us pilgrims as we journey together towards eternity and travel to our destination along the curved pathway of human life.

Missed Opportunities

Standing patiently in line, waiting for my turn to place my food order for a quick lunch, my eyes focused upon the person standing next to me, in uniform, wearing the sleek attire of a Michigan state policeman.

The small child infatuation with a policeman has never completely left me. The uniform continues to represent for me a symbol of remarkable courage, solid strength, and honored valor. You have to be tough and confident to survive in the business of law enforcement.

It is humbling to confess that it would be impossible for me to maintain my control over that fearful surge of intense anxiety that must arise upon an approach to the frosted covered driver's side window of a car stopped along the shoulder of an interstate highway in the early hours of the morning, or the closed front door on the porch of a house inhabited by a couple embroiled in a violent domestic dispute.

In my childhood memory is a police officer killed in the line of duty, a young man who was known to my parents, who came to my house one day to allow an impressionable boy to sit in the front seat of a police car, to activate the siren, to flick a switch and marvel at the lighted maze of swirling overhead lights. A few months later he was gone, forever.

There can be reasons to dislike a policeman. Behavior that is too forceful, displays of authoritarian power and aggression, the use of unnecessary physical force while making an arrest, or harassment of a person profiled by features of an ethnic or racial group. There always will be examples of the bad mixed in the bundle with the good.

It was a comforting sense of protective security to observe his presence, wearing that crisply pressed and pleated uniform, the belt of distinctive work tools clasped around his waist, the traditional officer's cap perched upon his head, an identifying name tag worn above the fastened pocket of his shirt.

Why was that moment allowed by me to pass in silence without expressing my gratitude to that person standing alongside me in the line waiting to place an order for his lunch?

Message of Hope and Wisdom

A few years ago, with the assistance of a reputable internet service, I began to research and to explore the study of genealogy, identifying the names, dates of births and deaths, the spouses, children, and locations of migratory residences for my many ancestors.

I discovered that my research was reliable retroactive to the early 17th century on my maternal side, but shortened to only the early 19th century for my paternal or Italian ancestry. I carefully organized and then self-published a small book to preserve a record of my findings for future generations of my descendants. I desperately wanted to avoid having the work product of my tedious genealogical research discarded or lost by the passage of time.

Until this effort was made by me, my awareness of any details about the lives of my ancestors was limited to my paternal and maternal sets of grandparents.

Indeed, I had never met or spoken with my Dad's parents and had no direct personal experience of them. My maternal grandparents were known to me, but I never had a meaningful substantive conversation with my maternal grandfather and considered my maternal grandmother, although beloved by me, to be an aged relic from a bygone time.

My genealogical research reshaped my regard for my ancestors. I began to regret that I had no means or opportunity to have an interaction with the minds of my ancient ancestors, among whom were 17th century pilgrims to America, frontier pioneers, Revolutionary War veterans, Civil War battlefield casualties, and people forged by the toughest, the harshest, and the most brutal environmental obstacles and natural inconveniences imaginable.

I hunger for a conversation with Loomis Gray, my great grandfather, and his father, Ambrose, or John Gray who arrived aboard an ocean vessel in Boston harbor in 1637. His descendants, my great grandfathers many times removed, had enlisted in the Connecticut militia during the Revolutionary War.

Leroy Irick, my great grandfather, had migrated with his spouse, sons and daughters, from impoverished eastern Tennessee to Kokomo, Indiana, in the last years of the 19th century. Leroy's father and grandfather, Robert and Solomon, had fought bravely to preserve and to protect the Union, sacrificing their lives in battle during the Civil War.

The father of Solomon, a man named Michael Irick, had abandoned his infant son and twin sister, Polly, to the care of relatives after their mother and his spouse died from complications she had experienced during the labor of their births. How sad and difficult that decision must have been for him.

On my paternal side, the families had been residing in the central mountains of Italy for many centuries. My grandfather departed from the protective and parochial environment of his cloistered village nestled in the valley of the Matese Mountains, leaving temporarily and returning sporadically in pursuit of a "better life" economically for his spouse and children who remained in Italy.

While in America, my grandfather Rocchio earned modest wages in exchange for his toil in the most demanding and most exhausting manual labor jobs available to Italian immigrants arriving at the gates of Ellis Island. Details of his life remain hidden in obscurity and forever beyond the reach of my genealogical research, but I am certain that given the opportunity he would have compelling life stories to share with me. My life is diminished by his eternal silence.

My purpose in composing and publishing a personal memoir, to be read with affection by my family now living and by future descendants whose faces I never will be allowed to see and whose hands I never will be able to hold, is to make available to them the opportunity to experience the basic essence of who I was during my brief time alive on earth.

We humans have advanced and progressed at an exponential pace following the creation of the means for transmission of both acquired technical knowledge and profound personal experiences across generations, by use of language, either spoken as oral history or preserved in printed words. Whether we benefit from such a rich resource is a choice to be made by each of us.

I do know that were it possible for an invitation to be extended to me I would accept without any hesitation or doubt the opportunity to read thoughtfully the words of my ancestors, their sharing of the wisdom of experience, wrapped for me inside the gifted package of a personal memoir.

Don't Try to Stiff Your Paper Boy

My business career commenced at age 9, in late December, 1956, when I began my first paper route delivering the *Kokomo Tribune*. My route began on South Jay Street, south of Markland Avenue, and extended straight south, intersecting Foster and Virginia Streets, and continuing onward until the end of Jay Street, nearby the north side of the building then occupied by Delco Radio.

The average number of customers on my paper route could vary slightly, but usually approximated 100 households. In those years, the paper was delivered to nearly every house in the city and surrounding residential areas. Indeed, the proud *Tribune* masthead boasted that it was "Number One in Circulation Penetration" in the entire country, with every person reliant upon the paper for delivery of local, state, and national news.

The *Tribune* was delivered late afternoon on weekdays, and mornings on both Saturday and Sunday. Unless snow prohibited it, my preference was to load a canvas bag of folded papers onto my handlebars and while riding my bike steered and balanced solely by my left hand, I would use my right hand to throw the paper onto the front porch at each house on my compact neighborhood route.

Not to be vain, but it is true that I developed near perfect accuracy with my throws; if I occasionally missed a porch, I would stop, lower the kickstand, leave my bike, retrieve the misplaced paper, and drop or throw it onto the front porch. Guaranteed customer satisfaction required no less from me.

When severe weather conditions prohibited travel by bicycle, I would walk the route, carrying the canvas bag on my left side, supported by a strap placed over the right side of my neck and shoulder, freeing my right arm to enable me to throw the paper onto the porch from the sidewalk.

I delighted in passing papers in the early evening, after setting of the sun and the arrival of dusk. There would be the simple pure enjoyment of a pleasant aura of peaceful tranquility interrupted only by the shrill squeaking of winged bats circling in flight above and around the shaded bulbs of illuminated street lamps.

Every Friday after completing delivery of the papers I would remain on my route and begin the task of collecting the weekly subscription fee of 40 cents from each household. Most would anticipate my weekly front door knock and visit, and have the change available in a small glass dish placed nearby for easy retrieval.

With an average of 100 houses to be visited to collect for the cost of the daily paper, I always appreciated a customer who was punctual and prepared to assist me with achieving time efficiency in completing the collection process. However, on the bitterest cold and harsh windy days during the winter months, I never refused an invitation to step inside the front door for a few seconds to warm my frigid fingers.

Delivering the newspaper was a prized business venture for any boy who had the good fortune of securing a route. I do not recall any girls having paper routes in the late 1950s and early 1960s in Kokomo. Our community's perception of activities appropriate for girls in those years was very different from today's more inclusive and relaxed views of propriety.

Most every customer would pay on a regular weekly basis for delivery of the daily paper. By noon on Saturdays, each paper boy would visit the busy circulation department in the *Tribune's* offices at the corner of Mulberry and Union Streets, and pay an invoice equivalent to 30 cents for each customer, thereby allowing for 10 cents of the cost of each subscription to be retained by the route carrier as the profit earned from his labor.

It was mandatory for each paper boy to pay the Tribune on a weekly basis the 30 cents owed for each subscription regardless of whether a customer had paid for that week's delivery. The "risk of financial loss" was an uncertainty imposed upon each paper boy, adding an incentive for assuring a front door personal visit to each household to obtain collection of the subscription fee.

If a person moved and departed with a balance owed for past weeks of delivery, I would find a means to identify the former customer's new or relocated residence and visit him or her repeatedly to collect the delinquent subscription fee. It was always a very bad idea to try and stiff your paper boy.

I received a doctoral level education in the study of human nature from my exposure to and encounter with the various personalities displayed by the diverse customers residing on my daily paper route in Kokomo. The lessons learned have been a benefit to me during the years of my adult life.

Best Friends, Forever

This is the time of year when it is appropriate to become serious about Detroit Tigers baseball and believe fervently that this season's version will go all the way to the World Series.

Since the beginning of my memory, my favorite baseball team has been the Detroit Tigers. At the age of two, my best friend was a transplant from Detroit, and within a few years of our faithful friendship he introduced me to Tigers fever. Life has never been the same since the Tigers became my team.

The most treasured items in my youthful possessions were baseball cards featuring players on the Tigers roster.

My mind can recall instantly the picture printed on the face of the baseball cards for players prominent in my youth, including Paul Foytack, Billy Hoeft, Bill Tuttle, Frank House, Al Kaline, George Kell, Harvey Kuenn, Frank Bolling, Charley Maxwell, and Ray Boone.

No place on earth can match the thrill of entering Tiger Stadium for the first time. What a glorious shrine to the game of baseball. However, Comerica Park is a fitting replacement, with its splendid assortment of Tiger history displayed proudly around the interior concourse and exterior walkways, including plaques, statues, and other reminders of the greatest players to wear the uniform of the Tigers.

My best boyhood friend died tragically in a freakish accident during our freshman year of college. My loyalty to our beloved Detroit Tigers keeps his spirit alive and shining in my heart.

Oh Danny Boy, this season's for you. A seat will be saved for you next to me at the World Series in Detroit. Best friends always sit together.

Anything's Possible

Let it not be the epitaph inscribed on my tombstone that here lies a man who could not sing a note and never mastered the art of playing a musical instrument.

The smooth singing of the lyrics of an inspirational song and the joyful playing of a stringed instrument producing the harmonious notes of a spiritual hymn are activities uniquely performed by humans, alone. But, there are those of us who must be branded as misfits for we lack the capacity to produce by use of our voice or fingers the sounds of music.

My mind has an empty black hole occupying the spot where music resides in the ridged crevices of the average human brain. Count me among those who are classified as tone deaf.

With a tuned guitar or banjo cradled in my hands, the sound repetitiously produced does not match the melody or lyrics of any sheet music produced in the history of the civilized world. The sound is something similar to a baby shaking a rattle. The tortuous tone of my excuse for singing is recognized only by a mating rhinoceros.

But, in the months ahead it shall be my unwavering goal to master the playing of a stringed instrument and to tame the vocal cords by singing the lyrics of a beautiful ballad. It may be too much to expect a Gene Kelly singing in the rain moment in my life, but my playing and singing music should not be the equivalent of pigs flying through the sky.

The certain attainment of my worthy musical goals shall be dedicated to all of those who share with me, that is before the development of the new musical me, the scourge of being unable to either sing the lyrics or play the melody of a single song. When we meet on the street, please sing softly your hello and goodbye.

Making Choices

There is some quality to fire that connects it in a very unique way to our distinctly human condition.

Fire conforms to the supreme principal of opposites, that magnificent governing rule of life on earth, by which every feature of human life has a non-identical twin with a totally opposite effect.

We have night and we have day. We have cold and we have hot. We have light and we have darkness. We have good and we have evil. We have sorrow and we have joy. We have hatred and we have forgiveness.

Sitting aside a wood or gas fueled fire burning in a fireplace situated in a comfortable and cozy family room is an enjoyable experience.

Gazing upon burning logs stimulates the activation of a natural relaxant chemical in our brain cells, creating a sense of mild euphoria.

Yet, the observation of a burning fire can be an alarming and disturbing experience, a frightening display of nuclear like power, an explosion that separates and releases energy from mass.

Fire can be destructive, violent, and vicious, as it scorches the earth, melting plant life and incinerating any human trapped in its pathway of destruction.

There is much about life around us that we cannot understand or explain with our limited vocabulary of words. Faith requires an exceptional act of trust, by which we accept the mysterious conditions of human life without protest.

As we choose to rise each morning and live each day we are pilgrims on a journey in search of perfect love. Every person has the capacity to love or to hate, to inspire or to condemn, to help or to hinder, to smile or to frown.

Our life can be the glow of a warm fire, radiating love, forgiveness, inspiration, hope and encouragement. Or, we have the freedom to choose a life filled with rabid acts and wanton thoughts producing acts of destruction, hatred, violence, and torture.

Ultimately, the quality of each human soul is defined not by riches or possessions but by the sum of the unique selections made daily by that person in choosing between opposites.

Rafting on the Wildcat Creek

Living my young years as a boy residing in Kokomo's near south east side neighborhoods I was aware of the impact of the presence of the Wildcat Creek which dissects the city creating an imaginary but very visible north and south boundary line.

For those of us in my boys' club or "gang," the south bank of the creek was the location for hours of adventurous play during the summer months. We would hike through the brush, fish with simple cane poles using earth worms for bait, climb up, across, and down the craggy edged boulders surrounding the vertical stone pillars supporting the Pennsylvania railroad trestle crossing the creek, and occasionally sleep in a tent made of old blankets we had assembled near the bank.

Our parents never displayed any worry or concern about our safety. All of us were protected by a form of surveillance somewhat unique to us, a "skill" acquired as a by-product of growing up in the toughened near south east side of Kokomo. That protection is called "street smarts" and it saved me from many potential risks.

We had an obsession with the idea of constructing a wooden raft and then lowering it with ropes onto the Wildcat Creek from a perch on the railroad trestle, above the streaming water below. We were successful many times in completing the building of our raft but never succeeded in lowering it onto the creek.

Indeed, after the frustration of many failed attempts to launch our raft onto the creek, my Dad and Uncle Frank decided to take over the project and develop a plan for a successful lowering of our raft from the overhead railroad trestle. The adults pushed the boys aside, excluded from the planning stage, and transported the raft onto the railroad trestle.

What followed was the only time I saw my Dad and Uncle Frank, his closest friend and brother, have a meltdown of shouting, insulting, and vociferously arguing about who was at fault for the disaster that had occurred in front of us.

Specifically, they were in the process of lowering the raft by use of rope pulleys when it broke loose, flipped, and crashed, splintering upon impact with the surface of the creek, sinking like a reenactment of the Titanic. Despite the presumed brilliance of my Dad and Uncle Frank we accomplished only another failed attempt to lower our raft onto the streaming water of the Wildcat Creek.

Of course, it is not possible to travel on a raft on the Wildcat Creek without successfully launching the raft onto the creek. Our dream of drifting on our raft along the Wildcat Creek, to the Wabash River, to the great Mississippi, was never fulfilled despite our group commitment to the adventurous project.

Today, I occasionally come across a print media or video advertising classic paddleboat cruises departing regularly from ports along the Mississippi River, primarily marketing to the senior citizen population which presumably has the money and time to invest in a river cruise.

Those advertisements are not effective with me. Taking a paddleboat cruise on the Mississippi River in a lavish bedroom suite with a private balcony view, evening entertainment in the form of song and dance, feasting on a never ending buffet of delicious chef prepared food; that pampered and frilly experience would never satisfy me.

I want a ride on a wooden raft, flowing along the Wildcat Creek to the Wabash River, eventually reaching and entering onto the historic Mississippi River. That experience would satisfy me, I think, maybe.

Wildcat Creek

Boss of My House

In my homestead the week after Thanksgiving is a predictable time of stressful disharmony, bitter discord, and stubborn disagreement.

In a chestnut, our problem is that we have serious differences of opinion regarding the correct day of the season for displaying the holiday decorations, putting up the Christmas tree, exchanging and opening presents, returning the holiday decorations to storage containers, and folding up for another year of hibernation our spectacular but artificial Norwegian evergreen tree.

My preference, not that it matters, is to get a quick and early start on the holiday season. Beautify the home with colorful displays of deep green holly and ivy, set out the miniature Dickens era village pieces populated by tiny figurines meant to resemble Scrooge, Marley, and Bob Cratchet, put on display that priceless family heirloom collection of blown glass ornamental reindeer placed in front of a snow white sleigh.

In my world, the Christmas tree would be released from the confinement of its storage box, have its branches spread, its bulbs hung, its lights strung, and be ready to welcome one and all bright and early immediately after breakfast the day following Thanksgiving.

Presents should be exchanged and opened on Christmas Eve, instead of the morning of Christmas day, with the exception possibly of a few costly or special gifts reserved for night delivery by Santa. After the celebration of Christmas Day, everything should stay as it is, including presents in boxes left under the tree, until the second week of January, at the earliest. Then we return to our normal routines.

Of course, that is not the way it is in my home.

You are allowed one quick guess for naming the person whose opinions and preferences govern and determine the selection of family holiday traditions in the Theresa Rocchio household.

The fact is the decorations never appear until two weeks before Christmas, the tree goes up the weekend before, all presents and gifts are opened on Christmas morning, and everything is taken down and put away the second day of the new year.

I can humbug about it all I want but it is what it is.

Bicycling Through the Neighborhoods

My bicycle is an extension of my personality. I bought it three years ago at a local store. It is the traditional classic bike, with pedal brakes, only one speed gear, no hand levers, large white sidewall tires, and a soft comfortable oversized seat. Not too impressive but it gets the job done.

Nothing else in life matches the emotional euphoria of a relaxed bike ride through the neighborhoods on a warm pleasant evening during the spring season. It's the best way to see and experience life in the city.

Years ago, I advised an unfamiliar newly arrived school superintendent to decline golf at the County Club on Wednesday afternoons and substitute in its place a bicycle ride around town, and most importantly, stopping to chat casually with moms and dads sitting on porches or standing in lawns along the way. That's the best way to learn how parents and taxpayers rate the quality of our schools and the proposals they will or will not support as voters.

This is the season when we rediscover the beauty and joy of the outside world, emerging from our long winter hibernation. It's exhilarating to escape the despair and depression of late winter cabin fever, replaced by the sounds of song birds singing, children playing games on the concrete drives, and couples strolling along the paths in our town's beautiful parks.

Today is the first day of the rest of your life. As the proverb says, "Let us be glad and rejoice in it." Roll out the bicycle, dust off the seat, and enjoy a riding tour around the city streets, encountering life as it should be experienced by us. Relaxed, observant, and appreciative of what we have.

Jan, Becky, Marsha, Sherrie and Me

My first "real" girlfriend was Jan Golightly, when we were students in the seventh grade at St. Joan of Arc school in Kokomo. Each grade at St. Joan of Arc was divided into two sections designated by the letters A and B in the alphabet. Since my last name began with the letter "R" I was placed consistently in the B section.

I do not recall my being aware of Jan's existence or presence at the school before my seventh grade year, although she had been enrolled at St. Joan of Arc every year, but assigned to the opposite classroom. Midway through the first semester of my seventh grade year I began to notice some changes taking place in my view of the world, namely taking note of the presence of girls. Adolescence began and with its arrival came the release of testosterone in my blood stream.

My initial awareness of Jan occurred when I would see her in the rear seat of her family's car when her mom was driving her, a classmate, Sandy Hughes, and Jan's older and younger sisters, Kathy and Fabian, to school in the morning. I was a patrol boy at the busy intersection of Jay Street and Markland Avenue, and if stationed at the northeast corner, I could see directly into the back seat and view Jan seated in the family car as her mom made a right turn at the intersection.

Usually, Jan's mom would slow the car on Markland Avenue as she approached and began the right turn onto Jay Street. As she slowed the speed of the car I had my best chance to see Jan sitting in the back seat, against the passenger side door. I would smile and she would smile, and our eyes would lock and at that moment I knew and she knew we were a perfect match, made to be together.

Problem was at the age of 12 both Jan and I were unclear about what exactly it meant to be a perfect match, made to be together. How? When? Where?

During lunch hour at the school, students would browse at the books in the library. That is where Jan and I advanced our relationship from glances as she sat in her car riding to school in the morning to an exchange of smiles sent from across the room used as the school library.

Soon the relationship further advanced by my telephoning Jan every weekday evening and conversing as long as our parents would allow us to reserve the family phone denying its use to others in our respective homes.

The next step in the linear advance of our maturing relationship was our behavior at the annual St. Joan of Arc school student roller skating party at the local indoor rink. Holding hands as we skated together around the oval floor, I got close to her body and detected a faint scent of perfume which prompted me to notice the beauty of her flawless skin.

I think among a list of the top ten amorous and innocently erotic moments of my life would be included the electric feeling I had while roller skating with Jan around the oval rink, holding hands, exchanging smiles, experiencing a type and level of seduction that was foreign or strange to me. I think my life probably changed forever that night.

As the winter faded and the spring arrived, Jan and I drifted apart and the flame of our forever relationship flickered out and succumbed to my new interest in life, namely Becky Rostron and a very close second place, Marsha Bailey.

Becky was a public school student who had been living in my neighborhood forever although I had not taken notice of her presence until that spring. I began to spend the early evening hours in April and May in Becky's back yard, joined with a group of neighborhood friends, including Marsha, playing casual games of badminton and whiffle ball, interspersed with conversation about whatever self-conscious boys and girls would discuss at the age of 12.

Most amorous for me was interlocking my fingers with Becky's fingers in a contest referred to as a Grecian knuckle lock. As we squeezed the other's fingers, our hands would move inward bringing me in close to her face and occasionally near her lips. I wanted to kiss her but I lacked the confidence to try. Her scent of perfume was an intoxicant, her smile was hypnotic, and her eyes were gorgeous. I was hooked on Becky and I eagerly planned a life forever together with her. Marsha exited my plans since I understood the meaning of the word bigamist.

By the end of summer I was no longer hanging out with Becky or the group of friends we shared only months before, in the spring. Becky and Marsha forgot I existed. We had moved in different directions and what had seemed as if it was meant to be was not to be. Instead, I became smitten by Sherrie Donoghue, the most beautiful and physically mature 13 year old girl in the eighth grade at St. Joan of Arc school.

Incidentally, although we were meant to be together forever, Sherrie and I were no longer a couple after we completed the eighth grade and graduated from St. Joan of Arc in late May, 1961. Our school lives diverged and we attended separate schools for the ninth grade. That was the end of our eternal relationship.

I attended the ninth grade at a public school, Elwood Haynes Junior High, and as fate would have it Jan, Becky, and Marsha enrolled there with me. How kind but fickle fate can be in life. Opportunity thus knocked again. But, only I was doing the knocking and they were not doing the answering. Older boys with a driver's license had an insurmountable unfair advantage on me.

The Correct Way

How will we celebrate this Memorial Day? There will be picnics, family outings, travel, and other forms of enjoyable recreational activities. It is wonderful to have an extended three day weekend. But there is much more. It is a day to pay tribute to those who served and sacrificed their lives as members of our armed forces.

There is no real excuse in life for failing to set aside the time for participating in an event that commemorates the true meaning and purpose of Memorial Day. Solemn celebrations are conducted throughout the weekend providing us with ample opportunities to gather as a grateful community and express our appreciation to those who lost their lives serving in our armed forces.

We hear it said so often that the words may have lost their meaning. It is said that he or she lost his or her life serving us, protecting us, defending us, as a member of our armed forces. But the loss of that precious life is very real and never forgotten for even a moment by the family members of those patriots.

By saluting our national colors, attending a ceremony in the downtown park, saying thank you to a veteran who symbolizes those who served and never returned home, we do our patriotic duty.

It is a day for us to remember respectfully those who said goodbye, fought courageously, bravely, and never returned home.

Life's Miracle

In the bright morning hours, as the sun's rays began to brighten over the western shore of Lake Michigan, north of Chicago, Jillian Grace Rocchio made her entry into our world, beginning her life earlier this day.

She is a beautiful baby, a pure infant, sweet, gentle, soft, precious. How else do we describe that mesmerizing effect that the fresh face of a newborn infant has upon us? All potential, all hope, each breath from her lips inspiring our faith in humanity, encouraging us to believe that life is good, that life is purposeful, that life is intended for each of us by God.

As her grandfather, my hope for Jillian is that she experiences love throughout her life, nurtured by the encircling embrace of her protective family, warmed by the caring smiles of her many friends, and instructed by teachers who value the reality of her eternal soul.

You are with us now, Jillian. Together, in this miraculous mystery of life, it seems today as if you have been present always in my life, in my thoughts, in my dreams. Already you have enriched my life, seeing your face, curling my finger around your finger, smoothing your wispy silk hair, caressing your soft skin, feeling the warmth of your breath upon my smiling face.

Life on earth is only the childhood of our immortality. Welcome, beautiful glorious Jillian to your earth, to your world, to your immortality. May you live your life on earth not as a human being having a spiritual experience but as a spiritual being having a human experience.

My Hollywood Experience

One of the proudest experiences in my life was being chosen for a major supporting actor role in two popular movies during my young adult years while serving on active duty in the United States Navy.

The first experience occurred while I was stationed in Newport, Rhode Island, in late autumn, 1972. A casting call was made for young male officers to audition for a role in the movie to be titled "An Officer and a Gentleman" starring Richard Gere and Debra Winger. It was a complete and unexpected surprise when I received a post-audition call from the casting director asking me to do a second reading from the actual script.

Apparently, I made a favorable impression on the right people and received an invitation to participate in the making of the movie. It was a wonderful and unique experience that I will never forget, particularly the nude scene with Debra Winger when we went off together on a drunken escapade intended to raise the ire and jealousy of Richard Gere!

The character I played in the movie was named Lt. Art Ready, and he was a Navy lawyer, a member of the Judge Advocate General Corp, as I was indeed during my brief duty station assignment in Newport. Incidentally, Newport is a fantastic city with a rich history and a superb ocean side location.

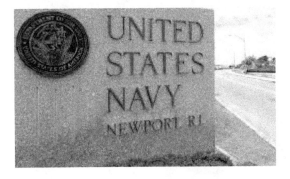

A few years later I was serving as a Navy lawyer in the western Pacific, assigned as staff judge advocate for Fleet Activities Okinawa. It was a memorable experience and gave me a lasting appreciation for the men and women serving in our armed forces. I have everlasting love for the Navy!

Anyway, by fate, I was invited during my time at Fleet Activities Okinawa to experience again, but only briefly, the excitement of having a role in a major Hollywood movie, titled "Top Gun," starring Tom Cruise in the lead actor's role. I had no experience as a naval aviator but the parts of the film which included me had me flying in the cockpit with and behind Tom Cruise in a real Navy fighter jet! What a great experience!

Tom Cruise was very friendly, polite and personable. I hung out with him and other members of the cast during that portion of the filming that took place onsite at the air facility maintained by Fleet Activities Okinawa. That segment of the movie took about three weeks to complete and it seemed like a party atmosphere every night after we broke from the working set and found ways to relax and to release our daily stressors.

Meg Ryan was another favorite of mine from the cast of my second movie making experience. We never developed a romantic connection but I do remember her as being rather flirtatious with me and I often remind my spouse, Theresa, that a famous actress had a crush on a younger, more handsome me! Theresa won't buy it but I keep trying to sell it to her!

I did not attempt to further develop a career as a Hollywood actor although I did receive some added offers from notable producers and directors during the years immediately following my discharge from active naval duty in early 1976.

My only real regret today was passing on the invitation to play the role of the family consiglieri (attorney) to Marlon Brando's Don Corleone in the epic film "The Godfather," which in retrospect would have been a once in a lifetime acting experience. Martin Scorsese was very gracious when I turned down his offer to be a member of the cast.

Life has its strange and unexpected moments, the twists and turns which present us with a problematic fork in the road and questions later about the path in the woods not taken in this meandering pilgrimage we walk along on this planet we call Mother Earth. The days come and the days go, just as today we celebrated the first day of the month of April, or as we say, happy April you know what day.

Clearing The Way

It might be appropriate for Hallmark Cards to promote the celebration of an annual event which recognizes the valuable and indispensable services provided by snow plow drivers. Is there any person more vital to the life of our community on the day following an overnight snow blizzard?

Doctors, accountants, bankers, teachers, and all other occupations and professions contribute to the commerce in our community but the effects of a snow blizzard would silent their activity and bring our economy to its knees without the crisis intervention of the fabled snow plow driver. Just imagine a world lacking snow plow drivers.

Of course, there also is a platoon of private citizens armed with plows mounted on the front of a truck who answer the call to duty on the worst of winter snow days.

This is life at its best. Who needs the pleasure of a walk on a sandy beach in a Florida retirement community, the excitement of snorkeling in a lagoon along the coastline of California, or a restful nap in the afternoon sun on a patio recliner in Hawaii? Not us.

We have the soothing hiss of a snow blizzard, soft cotton flakes dropping from the sky, a blanket of white fluff stretched across the yard, and, most importantly, that reassuring and distinctive symphony of sound orchestrated by our beloved snow plow drivers. This could be as good as it gets

Another Day In The Office

In the early morning before sunrise the day after Christmas, we lost electricity at my house. I was the first to awaken. Descending the stairs from the bedroom to the kitchen, I stood motionless as the lights went out and the house instantly darkened.

I made the call to the utility provider's emergency telephone number and reported the power outage. And, then I waited in the darkness for the dependable line repair worker to appear in the neighborhood, diagnose the problem, correct the outage, and restore electrical power to my house.

In less than an hour, the repair truck appeared on the street, crawling along the pavement, with its sole occupant searching carefully with his eyes, trying to identify the source of the outage, looking for a clue in the form of a fallen branch, a sagging power line, or a smoking transformer.

Within thirty minutes after the line repairman's arrival, the flow of power was restored to my house, and life quickly returned to our normal energy dependent routines.

My New Year's resolution is to live a work life that resembles the line repairmen who answer the call, appear day or night, in rain, snow or sleet, to do the job they have been called to do simply because that's their job.

No fanfare, no bonus in the pay envelope, no public accolades, only the example of a person doing what he or she is paid to do and doing it the right way simply because someone is depending upon him or her to do the job properly. That's a resolution worth keeping in the year ahead.

Minor Inconvenience Solved

After her graduation from college and arrival in Okinawa, Theresa and I began our life as a married couple in early June, 1973, making a home, although temporary, on a Pacific island located away from the emotional support of our families back in New Jersey and Indiana.

We had been inseparable for 11 days before we became engaged on a beautiful sunny Saturday afternoon in Newport, Rhode Island. After our wedding ceremony and a wonderful week for a honeymoon in Miami Beach, Florida, we separated as I embarked to Okinawa for duty as a Navy lawyer and she returned to Salve Regina College to complete the spring and final semester of her college education.

We lived in Okinawa for a few weeks beyond one year, leaving on July 2, 1974, a day after we celebrated my 27th birthday. The travel odyssey for our return to the United States is material for another story.

We rented a house with painted white exterior walls accented by red and black window trim colors. Modern Okinawan houses were constructed of cement or concrete to withstand the powerful forces of typhoon wind gusts. The neighbors surrounding us were all natives of Okinawa. They were friendly towards us and we communicated barely but adequately in the global language of head nods, hand gestures, and facial expressions.

Our house was furnished modestly with items and objects we had purchased at the base exchange or general store. Two wooden rocking chairs, a desk and companion office chair, a card table for our meals together, a set of folding metal framed chairs, a floor lamp, bed, dresser, and basic kitchen appliances.

Our car was a rather dilapidated and fatigued VW Beetle, whose odometer had stopped calculating mileage years ago. The vehicle had a history of being sold and transferred from owner to owner as people returning home to the states passed those arriving from the states. The person leaving no longer needed to have a car on Okinawa; the person arriving was in search of a car to drive on Okinawa. A few hundred dollars was paid as the bartered purchase price and the title certificate was exchanged without any warranty given, the car purchased "as is" by the buyer.

The VW leaked, dripping water profusely from the rusted rim of the sunroof situated directly over our heads, above the driver and front passenger seats. And, in Okinawa rain is plentiful. Storms can arrive suddenly and unannounced.

Typically, we spent our weekend days driving around the perimeter of the island, stopping at shops and stores to sample native foods and browse at souvenirs and more practical use merchandise. The scenery was fantastic. The ocean water was transparent, clear and clean, a glistening blue color, accented by growths of coral reefs.

To remedy the problem of driving in the rain, we determined that the best solution was to have in the back seat readily available to us, two pieces of clear plastic sheets which had been used as protective cover for our shirts, slacks, and blouses returned to us from a local commercial dry cleaner or laundry.

When the rain began to fall, and the water started to seep from the sunroof onto our heads, we would cover our bodies from neck to feet with a piece of the clear plastic sheets, somewhat similar to use of a standard poncho. It was not a perfect solution but it was adequate for our needs.

When we departed permanently from Okinawa, the leaky VW Beetle was sold to an arriving sailor and his spouse, "as is," without warranty of fitness. I cannot remember today if I disclosed to the buyer the condition of the leaky sunroof. Still, I sleep soundly without the burden of guilt. We did leave the plastic sheets in the back seat of the car for use by the new owners.

Toy Guns and War Games

During my elementary school years, the 1950s, it was common for boys to receive toy guns as a birthday gift or Christmas present. Indeed, by my 12th and last innocent childhood birthday, I had accumulated an impressive coveted collection of authentic toy weaponry.

The popularity of toy guns was likely a product of a time when memories of World War II were fresh in the minds of American adults. My Dad, like many of the young dads in the neighborhood, was a veteran of the recent war, having fought with Patton's Third Army and the 65th Infantry Division in Europe. And, my Dad, like most dads in the neighborhood, never spoke about his actual wartime experiences to avoid refreshing dark memories that might unleash nightmarish images and horrific flashbacks recalling the inhumane savagery he had witnessed during those years.

We would muster as a group of boys, maybe 5 or 6 of us, randomly choose sides, and spread out to disperse across a 1 block area of houses, bounded by King Street on the north, Jay Street on the east, Harrison Street on the south, and Purdum Street on the west, a rectangular field outlined for our waging of war battles.

One side of the battle would search out and locate the other side. When a member of the enemy force was seen, imaginary gunfire would be exchanged and by use of a sacred honor code the dead soldier would be agreed upon with only a rare objection raised by the victim. The decedent would no longer participate and he would return to my back porch to await the arrival of other victims. The hunt would continue until all members of the losing side had been shot and "killed" by the victorious battle hardened warriors.

We could be expected to continue playing this version of war games for an entire morning or afternoon. When we dispersed throughout the neighborhood, we would take up sniper positions and hide behind shrubs, in accessible open garages, and behind rust coated fire barrels found alongside the path of the gravel coated alley used weekly by the city's trucks to collect our garbage and household trash.

Every boy owned a toy rifle, rubber bayonet, water canteen, and if your dad was a war veteran, your apparel would include his helmet or wool hat, backpack, and eating utensils. This might be only play but it was the real stuff.

Also, we enjoyed playing games of cowboys and Indians guided by the same concepts and rules of engagement applied to our mimicking of ferocious Pacific or European war battles, always won by the patriotic and brave American soldiers and their loyal allies.

All of us had a set of six shooters, placed in holsters hung from the waist, and some of us wore cowboy boots, adorned by a set of two shiny spinning spurs attached to and extending from the rear of the left and right heels. Some wore cowboy style shirts and authentic hats to complete the apparel theme for playing Indian war games.

The cowboys always finished as the victors in their clashes with the savage Indians. There was never an exception made to that constant lifelike rule. The Indians always lost.

Today, it is most unlikely that boys in the modern American neighborhood entertain themselves by playing imaginary war games with play rifles and guns. Indeed, my two sons never had a toy weapon of any kind --- gun or knife.

It does seem rather inappropriate that we boys frequently played imaginary games that allowed us to discharge our imaginary weapons loaded with our "real" imaginary bullets, and in an imaginary but real life sort of way, kill our friends as required by our consensus rules of engagement to win our imaginary games of merciless search and destroy missions, much like some of us did for real years later in the thick jungle brush, the mud colored streams, the flooded rice fields of Viet Nam, life imitating child's imaginary play.

Taking the Day Off

My Dad believed in maintaining perfect attendance in performing his job as a foundry furnace operator at a factory then known as Haynes Stellite during my youth.

He worked continuously despite both painful debilitating bone fractures and the most brutal weather conditions. With a cast on his ankle and foot, he never missed a day of work and he overcame a winter storm that clogged the roads by walking in a foot of snow the two miles from our house to the factory.

For a few years during my late elementary school days, my Dad put in two shifts each day. After returning home from a day on the furnace in the foundry, he would share a meal with the family and then leave to spend the remainder of the day working as a bartender at a tavern he had purchased and operated on the south side of the courthouse square in Kokomo.

The above examples should be sufficient to convey the message clearly that my Dad had an exemplary work ethic. In exchange for a day's pay, he always felt obligated to furnish more than a day's work.

My first year of college was followed by a summer job working at the factory where my Dad was employed. Summer employment was not optional for me. My earnings were necessary to contribute to the funding of the costs of my college education.

My Dad worked the first shift from 7:00 a.m. to 3:30 p.m., and I worked the second shift beginning at 4:00 p.m. until 12:30 a.m., weekdays and occasionally on Saturdays. The scheduling arrangement enabled me to chat briefly with my Dad as he exiting from the factory and I was waiting for the whistle signaling the start of my shift.

In July of 1966, we experienced a blistering heat spell coupled with severe high humidity in Kokomo. The temperature measured in excess of 100 degrees for a string of days, at least for a solid week, and my job was performed in the brutal Rough Grind department which featured an environment which resembled the inside of a blast furnace.

One day during that exceptionally hot week I decided, imprudently, to take a day off and remain at home. I am sure that my Dad was concerned when I was not present for our usual daily chat as he exited from the factory. When he arrived home that day, he discovered me sitting in a chaise lounge situated in the shade under the branches of a tree in the back yard. I likely was sipping a cold frosty bottle of Stroh's, my preferred lifelong brand of beer and was listening to my portable radio.

My Dad was not pleased that I had chosen to miss a day of work and the earnings I thereby would forfeit by my absence. His displeasure was expressed by the disappointment he displayed on his face as he stood at the bottom of the chaise lounge, staring at me, hoping to coax an explanation from me that would explain my apparent display of disrespect for his work ethic.

I remember telling my Dad that it was "just too hot" to work that day. And, I recall him responding that life does not operate that way. His son would not be a person who would choose to take a day off whenever it might seem convenient for me to avoid the harsh conditions of life.

He instructed me to get out of my lounging chair, immediately, and sit in his car parked at the curb. He went into our garage and removed a few tools, including a hefty sledge hammer, pick, and shovel, and he placed them in the trunk of the car. We then proceeded to drive a few blocks to a rental house owned by my Dad, where he was in the process of tearing down and replacing the cement steps and front porch.

My Dad instructed me to exit the car, remove the tools from the trunk, and he informed me that he would return in 8 hours at the end of my "substitute work shift" after toiling that evening breaking up the cement and transporting the heavy chunks to a pile for later removal from the property.

As he had promised, my Dad returned for me in 8 hours, near midnight, and drove me home from the work station where he had deposited me earlier that day, in the late afternoon while the sun still shined hot and bright in the sky. When he drove up and arrived for me, I was dirty, my clothes soiled and wet from excessive perspiration, and I could barely lift my tired arms above my waist.

I believe that my Dad always understood that I appreciated the lesson he taught me that day in the summer of 1966.

It's vitally important but really simple. No one is entitled to take a day off in this life we live on planet Earth. No one gets a free ride.

The Day Jimmy Rayl Died

This past Sunday Jimmy Rayl died. If you had lived your adolescent or teen years in Kokomo, Indiana, from about 1957 through 1965, then you had a personal connection to the legendary Jimmy Rayl.

My sixth grade year was my first being allowed to attend home basketball games in Memorial Gymnasium, sitting with my school friends. Our season tickets placed us in a tightly packed row near the top of the narrow, wooden, and wobbly bleachers designated as section 7.

Jimmy Rayl was the symbol, the summit, the epitome of Kokomo High School basketball. Those were the golden years of high school boys basketball in the Hoosier state, featuring fierce rivalries between communities represented by their hometown boys waging war in a game of basketball on a hardwood floor.

Kokomo was a member of the North Central Conference whose members were ranked among the largest in student population. Indeed, my class of 1965 numbered approximating 950 graduates, sitting tightly in a mass of folding chairs arranged in neat rows on the gym floor for our solemn commencement ceremony.

Muncie Central, Anderson, and Lafayette Jefferson were the conference members representing Kokomo's bitterest historic rivals. Other fabled conference members were Marion, Logansport, Frankfort, New Castle, Indianapolis Tech, and Richmond.

The standard gymnasium in the North Central Conference could seat about 7,000 spectators, all season ticket holders. Friday and Saturday nights in the cold winter months brought the community together, unified us as a big neighborhood, assembled to experience an unparalleled and uniquely Hoosier social event.

Every young boy in Kokomo wanted to be the next Jimmy Rayl. On the first warm day in the spring of 1959, with my Dad's guidance, I installed firmly in the hard soil along the south side of my home's detached garage, a stiff wooden plank post with a plywood backboard attached and an iron rim laced with a string net tightly bolted on it, measuring exactly a distance of 10 feet above the ground.

1959 was Jimmy Rayl's senior season, when he led his team to the state tournament's championship game in historic Butler Fieldhouse. Along the way, shooting his favorite jump shot from a distance of 30 feet or more from the basket, Jimmy Rayl was awarded both the prized Trester Attitude Award and the title of Indiana's Mr. Basketball.

So, I practiced, practiced, and practiced more until I was confident I would be the next Jimmy Rayl of Kokomo Wildcat basketball. I was indifferent to harsh weather conditions, be it driving rain, piercing sleet, blinding snow, frigid cold or blistering heat, Forrest Gump like I kept playing the game that would someday make me famous, just like the legendary Jimmy Rayl. I believed.

I never survived the varsity cut for the basketball team's roster at Kokomo High School. I lacked the talent, or at least the reflexes, the speed, the size, the instincts necessary to stand out in a school population numbering nearly 4,000 student members. There were a lot of good athletes who never made a team in those years in Kokomo.

Eventually, high school basketball, not unlike the demise of the hometown delivered daily newspaper, lost the hard battle to other activities competing for the community's leisure time hours on weekend evenings in the winter months. Gyms no longer filled to capacity, bleaches remained folded against the interior walls, and the bloated size of those proud community financed venues began to seem like misfit relics.

I still have my priceless memories of basketball in the golden age of Jimmy Rayl, Kokomo's Splendid Splinter, his uniform number 32 in the game program, forever number 1 in our hearts. His style and play made a contribution to my life, inspiring me to compete, to hope, to dream, to rise above disappointment and to recognize that the quality of my participation in the game of life will be the only score that really matters at the end.

Actually, there will never be a day when Jimmy Rayl dies in my life.

Papa Red, Jeanette, and Flavored Snow Cones

When I was a boy in my preteen and early adolescent years, there was a store located on the north side of East Vaile Avenue in Kokomo, nearby the heavily traveled Pennsylvania Railroad tracks passing across the paved street surface in the form of parallel lines stretching in a north and south direction.

My best recollection is that the store had no name. We, simply, identified it as the place belonging to and managed by Papa Red and his spouse, Jeanette. The inventory offered the browsing buyer a limited variety of basic foods such as canned soups, loaves of bread, soft drink beverages, and an assortment of candy and sweets.

Top of my list were the seasonal snow cones consisting of crushed ice packed into a paper cone and flavored with an abundant squirt of flavored syrup from an upside down glass jug, strawberry, orange, and grape being our favorites.

Also, Papa Red and Jeanette offered a sparse menu with very limited selections available for diners taking a seat in either of the two window side booths. The house special was a cheeseburger flavored with a generous slice of onion, a cut of succulent deep red tomato, embellished by a melted thick slice of pure Wisconsin cheddar cheese.

Most customers visiting the store came from the immediate neighborhood which meant that Papa Red and Jeanette barely reaped a modest profit from hours of daily labor which usually consisted of sitting on a stool, occasionally frying a hamburger on the kitchen grille, stocking the shaky shelves, and pouring a small sized fountain drink for me and my group of friends purchased at a cost of a single nickel. There was no change to leave for a tip.

The interior of the store was blazing hot in the summer due to a lack of air conditioning and alternatively frigid cold in the winter due to a malfunctioning antiquated furnace.

Those undesirable and harsh conditions never affected the friendly welcome always extended by Papa Red and Jeanette when the arrival of our boisterous gang was signaled by the opening of the squeaky hinged front screen door.

Papa Red and Jeanette were exceptional practitioners in both the art of observation and the skill of listening. They were never critical or dismissive of us despite our immaturity, our youth, and our lack of real world experience.

They were, simply, good people whose daily presence made my near south east side neighborhood a better place to live than it would have been without them and the positive influence they exerted upon me in my formative adolescent and preteen years.

Good people do make a difference, in simple but lasting ways.

Preserving Middle Class Jobs

A show on the Discovery channel is titled How It's Made. Each half hour segment displays and describes the process of manufacturing a product that is a popular and common feature of modern life in America, such as popcorn, golf clubs, steel wool, and automatic dishwashers.

It's fascinating to learn how brilliant mechanical engineers have designed the machinery necessary to manufacture products on a mass scale. Using an assembly line approach, special purpose machines punch out thousands of flawless items per day, often without significant human input.

Is there a progression point in our technological advancement where we recognize that the impressive efficiency of the machinery that performs tirelessly without the distractions inherent in human behavior also costs a human life an opportunity to perform a manufacturing job in exchange for a living wage?

Not everyone is going to earn an income by performing a service sector job, filling the positions of lawyer, doctor, banker, accountant, office administrator, fast food cook, travel agent, or retail clerk. Indeed, the very survival and future existence of the American middle class depend upon availability of good paying manufacturing jobs. Our middle class is now an endangered species.

Restoration of the American middle class depends upon rediscovering our nation's capacity to manufacture products utilizing not only machinery but also the efficient use of human labor. That's what America truly needs and that's everyone's job to encourage its accomplishment.

Labor Needs Its Voice

The Department of Labor has made a decision to include those who have been unemployed for more than two years in the monthly count of the unemployed in our country.

Apparently, before that decision was made last week, those who remained unemployed for more than two years were regarded by the statisticians as being persons with no interest in seeking an employment position. That belief may accurately describe some people but it certainly does not apply to most people involuntarily grouped in the category of the chronically unemployed. The voice of the voiceless should be heard.

In the stitched fabric of the quilt of the American community, we cannot afford to eliminate the presence of the middle class population. If we allow the middle class to become an extinct species, our nation will lose the guiding influence, moral strength, and the genuine patriotic fervor of those most responsible for the definition of the American dream.

The most authentic threat banging on our door is the beat of the drum counting down to the extinction of manufacturing in our national economy. In our local communities, from the shores of the Atlantic to the coast of the Pacific, we are losing manufacturing jobs by the minute.

Our national way of life will not survive without jobs paying wages sufficient to maintain the existence of a viable middle class in America. Forget about all the other concerns such as national health care, the war against terrorism, the bloating budget deficits, and the alarming decay of our infrastructure of bridges and roads.

We no longer will be America if our country's census count ceases to include a populous, vibrant and secure middle class. We need to restore and to protect manufacturing jobs in America. It is a simple fact that should be the primary concern of every local, state, and national politician elected and sworn by solemn oath to represent the best interests of us, the American people.

Respect

My dad, Benedetto (Benny) Rocchio, began working as a foundry furnace operator at the Haynes Stellite factory on Lindsey Street in Kokomo in 1938. With the exception of his active duty military service during World War II, he continued performing that same job until he retired in 1977 at the age of 62 years.

Between my first and second years of college, I spent the summer employed at the same factory where my Dad was employed, although he worked the first shift and I worked the second shift. There was a brief overlap between the end of his shift and the beginning of my shift, and those minutes allowed us to meet each day as he departed and I arrived at the plant.

My Dad operated an extremely hot furnace in the foundry section of the plant. Remarkably, he had a perfect attendance record when he retired in 1977. That accomplishment was an extreme rarity. His reliability was appreciated by both his co-workers and his supervisory personnel.

At the end of each shift, my Dad would be covered with soot and soaked with perspiration. And, each day before he exited from the plant grounds he would take advantage of the private showers provided for use by employees, located adjacent to and nearby an open area filled with lockers for use by an employee during his shift for the storage of small items of personal property.

As my Dad made his exit from the factory each day and returned home, he would be wearing a clean shirt, pressed slacks, black dress shoes, accompanied by a slightly detectable scent of his Mennen brand after shave lotion.

My Dad had a huge dosage of self-respect unlike any other person known to me, both then and now. In my middle aged years I encountered a quotation that I believe summarizes his approach to both his job in the factory and his appearance when outside the plant before and after his workday shift. It states as follows:

"If a man is called to be a street sweeper, he should sweep streets as Michelangelo painted, Beethoven composed music, or Shakespeare wrote poetry. He should sweep so clean that all the voices of heaven and earth will pause to proclaim that here lived a man who did his job well."

That pretty much summarizes my Dad and his admirable work ethic which enabled him to have his equally admirable sense of self-respect.

Cycle of Life

There are two predictable events that recur in our lives each day, often overlooked or disregarded by us in our daily routines.

The first is the event of a sunrise. Its glorious rays welcome us to the beginning of each day. A sunrise unfolding on the eastern horizon makes available to us an opportunity to witness a truly spectacular and miraculous event absent any price for admission.

Each sunrise begins with the appearance of a burst of soft, diffuse yellow rays, announcing the arrival of a brilliant ball of glowing yellow, followed by its reliable progression upwards in the sky to its restful perch above us.

We gather our energy each day from the presence of the sun. It reminds us that each morning is a new beginning, proclaiming the arrival of opportunity to recast who we are, what we value, and what we desire from ourselves and others. In the words of the sacred psalm, let us be glad and rejoice in this day which has been made for us.

It is perfectly appropriate that the instrument which proclaims the beginning of each day is also the tool that signals the passing of each day of our lives. Life is greatly influenced by the presence of opposites, and so it is that the descent of the sun below the horizon of the western sky announces the completion of another day in our life cycle on earth.

Too often we find the way in our daily life to look past and beyond the natural occurrences whose presence reminds us that nature is majestic, powerful, and brilliant. Good surrounds us but we must make the decision to allot the time to be observant and recognize its forms of expression in the environment of our daily lives.

Very Important Person

As an adult male and father of five adult children, my perspective on motherhood is biased and subjective. Obviously, I have never been a mother to children, but in my childhood I did benefit from having a wonderful mother and I have been blessed to live my adult life with a woman who is a perfect mother to my children.

I doubt that we men can ask for anything more than to be so fortunate as to have had the double blessing of a caring mother present during our childhood and a loving spouse for our children during our adult years. Male parental rights issues aside, my mind harbors no doubts whatsoever about which parent is rated most influential, beloved, and cherished by my children.

When adult age children call home, always that communication is directed to Mom, not Dad. Information about what is going on in the family circle is the domain of the mother queen. To exchange information about siblings, cousins, aunts, uncles, and Dad, too, the source of all news that is worthy of knowing is Mom, and Mom alone. What's Dad got to do with it?

The gender of the child makes no difference to the preferential selection of the child in preferring Mom over Dad. My sons, at heart, are Momma's boys. My daughters, at heart, are Momma's girls.

But, motherhood is not the easiest job in America. Indeed, in today's world of conflicting priorities and competing time demands it may be the most difficult job on planet earth.

This year after we have offered our praise to those important women in our life on Mother's Day, keep in mind that on those other 364 days of the year real life mothers and their children benefit from our expressions of appreciation, our offering of a helping hand, and our understanding that it is for many women a daily struggle to be a really good Mom.

Being Together Now and Forever

My Dad, after his marriage to my Mom in 1939, lived his entire adult life in Kokomo. They resided until their respective deaths in 2009 and 2013 in the same residence they first occupied as a newly married couple after returning from their honeymoon. With the help of a carpenter, the house was built solely by my Dad in anticipation of his upcoming marriage.

Before his marriage, my Dad did move about somewhat, including a stint in the Civilian Conservation Corp assigned to planting saplings in California forests. He had a brief experience as an apprentice tailor while residing temporarily with friends in Cincinnati, Ohio.

Eventually he returned to Kokomo and rekindled his relationship with my Mom, culminating in their marriage at St. Joan of Arc Catholic Church on November 18, 1939. At the time of her death in early 2009, they had been married for a total of sixty nine (69) plus years.

My parents were inseparable with the exception of my Dad's active duty service in the United States Army in World War II, when he fought with the 65th Infantry Division in Germany. On the day of his death in 2013, my Dad was the oldest surviving member of the Division. He remained so trim and physically fit that he could wear his Army dress uniform!

My Dad made some attempts to work as a stone mason, a tailor, and a factory machine operator until eventually he settled on an employment position as a foundry furnace operator at Haynes Stellite before he was drafted into the Army in late 1943.

He returned to his job at Haynes Stellite (later named Union Carbide) after his discharge from the Army and he remained employed as a foundry furnace operator until his retirement in 1977.

My Mom not only loved my Dad but also she loved his brothers, their spouses, and children. She never appeared resentful or annoyed by the Italian heritage embraced by her foreign born spouse. Indeed, she had converted to his Roman Catholicism to facilitate their marriage and to assure him that she would concur with his belief that their children must be instructed in the faith of his ancestors, by attending Catholic elementary schools.

My parents enjoyed a supportive and beautiful marriage, together as spouses for almost 70 years living in their only home, on Jay Street, in Kokomo, Indiana. They were honest, loyal, caring, and devoted to their marriage and their children.

Snowflakes

It's not easy, living the life of a snowflake. If anyone thinks my life is simple and uncomplicated, they are mistaken.

People believe that snowflakes are identical in appearance. In fact, there are no two snowflakes alike. We have our distinctive characteristics and unique features, although at first glance it might appear that there are no real differences in our shapes and forms. If you look closely, you will see that every snowflake has its very own and individualized special structure made of frozen water crystals.

When you are a snowflake, you have to adjust to cold temperatures, and often bitterly cold weather. The environment in which we snowflakes exist is not ideal, but we have no choice about where we form and where we land when we drop from the sky and arrive on earth.

And, all of us, we instinctively sense that our time is limited, and we know that soon we will disappear when the warmth of the midday sun shines brightly, transforming us into water and vapor. All snowflakes share that same destiny, and we do not allow the unknown of our future to diminish the joy of our life now.

Snowflakes are by nature social creatures. We have our best days when we join with other snowflakes and produce the spectacular scene of glistening limbs on an otherwise barren tree, sparkling ivory colored jewels adorning a lit lantern post at night, or the soft white blanket covering frozen waves along a Lake Michigan shore.

It is a challenging but satisfying existence, being a snowflake. It may often seem that there are too many of us taking up space, but if you look closely, you will recognize that each snowflake is a majestic expression of the natural beauty that abounds on the landscape of a tranquil and peaceful earth.

The Neighborhood Gang

When I write about my neighborhood "gang" of my youth, it is important to understand that I am not referring to a roving band of young delinquents or vicious criminals.

Simply, in Kokomo, in the 1950s and early 1960s, the word which would have been selected to describe a group of 3 or more young friends regularly hanging out together would be the word "gang," without its modern day negative connotations and definitions.

If nothing else defined the near south east side of my youth, it would be that every other house on the streets had a boy within 2 years, up or down, of my age. In an area enclosed by 6 streets running north and south and 4 streets extending east and west, there lived within that demographic rectangle the following:

Mike McHale, Kenneth Gleason, Tommy Gonzales, Albert Gonzales, Louie Arredando, Larry Perryman, Sandy Lowe, Mike Garro, Donny Smith, Danny Ross, Jackie Herron, Roger Herron, Jack Smith, Denny Camden, Jim Walton, Richard Elliott, John Bizjack, Jackie Featherstone, Jeddy Deets, Jerry Ogle, Chris Hagel, Keith Snow, Pasquale (Patsy) Rocchio, Jim Bowman, John Wiles, Mike Newburn, Bobby Newburn, Jim Rourke, Lanny Rourke, Tom Hamilton, Jim Hamilton, Pete Cone, Chuck Cone, Denny Etter, Mike Cunningham, Mark Shellenberger, Mike Shellenberger, and Jesse Gonzales.

Also, add the legendary name of Chuck Woolley as "The Fonz" of our neighborhood streets.

I am absolutely certain that the above is an incomplete roster but the list contains only the names that I now remember at this moment in time. Give me 2 minutes more to explore my memory, and I likely would produce at the very least another 5 names, possibly 10 or more. We had a lot of boys in the neighborhood.

Were there also girls? Of course, and likely their numbers were similar to the boys living within the boundary defining city streets of my near south east side neighborhood. But, until puberty entered the hormone stream of my circulatory system, girls did not count and they were excluded from our boy exclusive gangs.

Summer days of play and games would start soon after the beginning of daylight when I would depart from home after breakfast, remain away except for brief returns for lunch and supper, then promptly resume and continue until the curfew hour coinciding with sunset and the arrival of darkness on the streets.

Our informal kids-only play would involve seasonal appropriate sports, including tackle football, sandlot baseball, playground basketball, and swimming at the popular municipal pool located a bike ride away across town on the near west side.

It was simple to gather a sufficient number of friends for sports without any advance arrangements made to assure a favorable turnout. Just walk from house to house and invite participation in whatever sport was on the menu for the day.

There were no cars, except the impressive car driven around the streets by Woolley. It featured decibel destroying double mufflers, bubble rear skirts, rear mud flaps, and some unremarkable item dangling from the post used to mount the front window rear view mirror.

Bicycles were the preferred and only means of mobility except for walking. Literally, every boy had his bicycle which was treated with the respect given a cowboy's horse in the untamed Wild West of the American 19th Century.

My neighborhood gang life is replaced today by parent arranged play dates, travel sports leagues, adult supervised sports, and summer day or stayover themed camps. But, the modern equivalents seem unavoidable due to the demographics of today's neighborhoods; there are a lot less kids living in the houses today.

Origin of Halloween

The first settler to inhabit and remain in what became our city was Horace T. Phileas. He arrived in the depths of a severe winter blizzard in early February, 1842, accompanied by only an old mule and a flimsy wagon brought with him from western New York, near Buffalo, on the south shore of Lake Erie.

Confronted by heavy snow cover and fierce winter winds, Horace decided to stay until the weather cleared. He built a sturdy but simple log cabin near the creek and settled in to wait out the winter.

Being in the upper Midwest, the weather remained terrible and did not improve until the last day of October. For almost eight solid months, Horace had been isolated within the cabin he had built to shelter him from the snow and wind. For food, Horace did manage to kill a bear that had fallen asleep outside his front door, and he survived the lengthy brutal winter only by eating a daily diet of bear meat.

When Horace emerged from his cabin on the last day of October, 1842, he covered himself with the fur skin he had kept from the bear he had killed, and placed it around his body and took the skull of the bear and placed it on his head.

When he opened the door of his cabin, Horace was startled to discover that another pioneer had arrived and built a nearby cabin for shelter. Horace walked to the neighboring cabin, knocked on the door, and as it opened he said to the greeter, "trick or treat."

Horace was very pleased to see a lovely young woman on the other side of the door when it opened in response to his knock. Understandably, she was startled by Horace's appearance, dressed as he was in the fur skin of a bear with a skull sitting upon his head. After introductions, and desperate for companionship, she invited Horace into her cabin, a year later they married, and a month thereafter Horace, Jr. arrived!

To commemorate the first meeting of our city's founders, we and the entire world celebrate Halloween annually and hear the traditional "trick or treat" greeting when we open our doors to visitors dressed in colorful costumes. Now you know the true story of the origin of Halloween.

Determination

If you awaken one morning, and you are startled to discover that you have transformed into a turtle, remember that it's not an easy task for a turtle to cross a road. Your very nature as a turtle works against you, and interferes with achieving your goal of traveling from one side to the other side of the roadway.

If you take that first small step forward, you risk failure. Those little legs do not move rapidly, and they require a lot of energy just to move one teeny step at a time, left right, left right, until the weight of that heavy shell on your back feels like it is crushing in upon you.

There are all sorts of obstacles on the way across the road. You could encounter a log, a vehicle, an animal, or another turtle with an attitude, all potential sources of problems that threaten to interfere with your progress as you work your way steadily across the road.

Besides, as a turtle, you have those doubts about yourself, those disturbing and distressing insecure thoughts that question your need for making this potentially dangerous trip across the road.

Maybe you cross the road because as a turtle you know there are few things in life that will match the euphoria you experience, that refreshing surge of exhilaration that happens only upon the achievement of a goal that seemed unreachable, and impossible when you took that first step forward from the other side of the road.

Always remember that life for a turtle is just a series of tiny steps forward, one at a time.

Deep Roots in Gallo, Italy

There is a small and ancient village located along the spine of the Italian peninsula placed midway between Naples and Rome, tucked within the stone filled rolling hills of a region known to its natives as the Matese mountains, whose highest elevation measures 6,730 feet at the peak of Mount Miletto.

The village name is Gallo.

According to local lore or legend, and a scarce historical record, Gallo acquired its name around 1620. It constitutes a part of the province of Caserta. In 1921, the village population peaked at a count of 3,417 inhabitants. The most recent census follows the trend of a steady decline, counting only 648 citizens.

Recent archaeological discoveries uncovered in 1979 revealed the presence of fossilized bones of a primitive human who had lived in or around the vicinity of Gallo about 700,000 years ago. The specimen has been named *Homo Aeserniensis*.

The earliest "modern" inhabitants of Gallo are referred to as Samnites. This scattered population was absorbed into the Roman Empire around 250 B.C. In the 7th Century the area became populated by Bulgars who had emigrated from present day Bulgaria.

The history of the Rocchio family roots is the history of the village of Gallo. Indeed, every Rocchio residing outside Gallo can trace her or his ancestral roots to that village.

I visited Gallo and Italy once during my life. The visit occurred in late May, 1985. I was accompanied by my parents, my sister, Jan, and her spouse, Stephen.

After arriving in Rome by an overnight flight, we traveled to Gallo by automobile, precipitously progressing on winding mountain roads until our eventual arrival at our destination. My Aunt Rosa was alive, and she greeted us on the patio adjacent to the beloved family home, then vacant but occupied temporarily by us during our vacation week in Gallo.

My Dad was never happier than our week in Gallo when he was able to lead our family on a guided tour of his childhood village. The scenery was beautiful. The air was pure. The darkened sky was ablaze with stars at night. I have an album filled with pictures to enable me to remember that epic family trip.

There are two (2) very vivid memories of my days visiting Gallo. I recall a black ocean traveler's trunk on the floor in a sparse second floor bedroom which was filled with pictures that had been sent by mail to my grandmother before her death in 1966 and continued thereafter to be received and collected by my Aunt Rosa.

How wonderful it would be to have possession today of that ocean traveler's trunk and its contents! Likely, it had been owned by my grandfather and it had been used by him in his travels to and from Italy. Its precious content as viewed by me was a rare pictorial archive of not only my immediate family but also my Dad's siblings, their spouses, and their children.

My other vivid remembrance of my trip to Gallo is that when I first stepped upon the patio at the family house which had been built by my grandfather, I began to weep, eventually reaching a crescendo of uncontrollable tearful sobbing.

I said nothing and I wanted only silence with my inner thoughts, focused on generations of the Rocchio family who had lived in that pristine mountain village for centuries before me.

I felt the presence of their eternal spirits in my soul that day.

Benedetto and Beulah's Ancestral Family Trees

My Dad, Benedetto, affectionately called Benny, was born on February 14, 1915, in Gallo. His father, Pasquale, was forty one (41) years old and his mother, Pasqua, was forty (40) years old when their last and youngest child was born on Valentine's Day in 1915.

My grandfather, Pasquale, was born on March 6, 1873. I never met or saw him during his lifetime. He died on March 30, 1941, at age sixty eight (68), six (6) years before my birth in 1947. I have possession of Pasquale's treasured Italian passport which contains his photo, the only likeness of him known to me.

My grandmother, Pasqua, was born on January 30, 1875. She lived her entire life in Gallo, and died there on November 21, 1966, at the age of ninety one (91) years.

My Dad departed from Italy and immigrated to the United States in 1932, making the cross ocean voyage alone at the young age of seventeen (17) years. After arriving in New York harbor, likely at Ellis Island, he continued his travel to Kokomo, Indiana, where his uncle Giuseppe was residing and likely working as a stone mason assigned to the construction of a new factory building.

After he departed Gallo and traveled to the United States, my Dad returned only once to Italy to see his mother alive. That memorable trip home by him occurred in February, 1962. Before my Dad could return again to Gallo, his mother died in 1966, and is buried or entombed with her spouse in the family vault located in the village cemetery.

My Mom, named Beulah Irene, was born in 1919, in Kokomo, Indiana. Her parents were Cadle Irick, born in 1892, and Rosie (Gray) Irick, born in 1896.

My Mom was a middle child in a sibling group of three daughters. Her older sister was Phyllis, born in 1918; her younger was Ruth, born in 1925.

My Mom was a bright and intelligent woman, a loyal and faithful spouse, and a caring, nurturing mother to my sister, Jan, and me. Simply, she was a good person. Photos of her in her teen years always display Mom as having a lovely smile, a perky grin, and a bit of mischievousness hidden in the sparkle of her eyes.

Battered by the Great Depression, Mom discontinued high school early in her sophomore year to begin working in a factory to add needed income to the family budget. Later, as a middle aged woman, she obtained her GED and she was very proud of that accomplishment.

Mom was close with her sisters during her adult years, but to a greater degree with Phyllis. Likely, Mom and Phyllis had contact daily and Mom would see her sister, Ruth, at least on a weekly basis.

Mom and Phyllis had married two men of Italian ancestry who were good friends, my Dad and my uncle Carl Bruno. In fact, Mom was introduced to Dad through Carl and Phyllis. I have no idea how Carl and Phyllis met and began dating before marriage.

In adhering to Italian and family tradition, my grandfather Rocchio's oldest son was named Giovanni and his first daughter was named Caterina, to honor his parents. Carrying on that tradition, my first son is named Benedict in honor of my Dad, and, my son's oldest child is named Patrick, to honor me, his grandfather.

Much of Nothing

Everyone has stuff, and most likely too much stuff. It clings to our lives like flypaper on a wool sweater. Indeed, among my collection of stuff is a wool sweater, or two, or perhaps, three. It could be more.

Stuff is the articles, items, or objects which we either possess as the lawful owner or by an act of borrowing from an owner whose identity we no longer can remember due to all the stuff. As a matter of fact, all that mental stuff simply complicates the act of separating the stuff we own from the stuff we have borrowed.

No collector of stuff wants to throw stuff away, labeling certain stuff as lacking value, purpose, or use. You should avoid temptations about discarding stuff, and certainly prohibit your spouse, child, friend, or a bureaucrat from making decisions about your stuff. Never throw away any stuff. If you throw away stuff, you will regret it. It will be expensive to replace the stuff you impulsively discarded from your collection of stuff only to discover it is the exact stuff you need now as irreplaceable useful stuff.

Do not try to organize your stuff. If you add organization to stuff, you may forget where you placed or stored the stuff. Let stuff naturally collect and allow it to settle into a comfortable spot. You will intuitively know where it is and be able to locate it, when, if ever, you have a need for your stuff.

Hopefully, it has been helpful to you to learn about stuff from this essay on stuff. You may find it beneficial to retain these words and place them with your other stuff, just in case you have a need sometime in the future for this stuff.

Thank You for Your Service

All of us know someone who has served in the armed forces. It could be a sailor, an airman, a soldier, or a marine. Likely, the person you know is not a recipient of the Medal of Honor and never had a parade to honor his or her service to our country.

Why do we recognize every person who served in our armed forces with a national holiday named Veterans Day? Do we really owe the veterans among us an expression of our appreciation by designating a national holiday to honor them?

The answer is simple. Today you are not living your life under the stifling restrictions of a dictatorship, toiling in a slave labor camp, or reciting a mantra to a king. No one is telling you how to worship, what to read, who to admire, or what to do or not do with your life. You have the freedom or liberty to be you however you decide to shape and define the person represented by that special personal pronoun.

When you awaken on Veterans Day, reflect for a moment that the life you are about to experience today is made possible by the sacrifice of those who have served in our armed forces. The liberty to be you as you choose to define yourself is not a birthright given to every human living on this earth.

The type or quality of liberty we enjoy every day as Americans is a rarity. Millions of lives have been extinguished and sacrificed to enable you to have the freedoms you will experience today. Every veteran of our armed forces is a symbol of those who have died in defense of our liberties.

Expressing your appreciation to the veteran you know is the best way to say thank you to every person who is serving or has served to give you the opportunity to be you. It might be a parent or grandparent, an aunt or uncle, a cousin, brother or sister, neighbor, friend, or an acquaintance. You know someone who is a veteran.

Don't remain silent on Veterans Day. Speak up and say thanks. It's the right and respectful salute to be given by every American on Veterans Day.

Too Busy To Be Clean

There are those who experience sleepless nights, tossing and turning under the woolen blanket covers, perspiring onto the fleece pillow case, unable to fall asleep, taunted by painful thoughts of corrosive winter road salt, dirt and grime eating into the glossy paint finish of the car parked in the driveway or garage.

For that group living among us, a weekly visit to the corner car wash is a must do task. Indeed, a daily drive through cleaning at the deluxe price rate, which includes scrubbing of the wheels, front and rear bumper, hood and trunk, complete with an application of an organic ingredient car polish applied to every exposed inch of paint surface, seems to represent the most effective way to purify, protect, and maintain the vehicle's shiny exterior.

And, then of course, there are those of us who just prefer to surrender to the effects of road salt, dirt, and grime pasted onto the front, sides, and rear surfaces of our cars. There are deer roaming in the woods circling my home, and the hungry herd often visits my driveway to have a lick of that tasty flavored surface on what to their wondrous eyes should appear as a salt lick placed upon four rubber tires.

Frankly speaking, my frame of mind belongs to people who have a blind spot with regards to a need for cleaning, waxing and polishing a pickup truck or car. Why bother, anyway.

The inside of my car is littered with fast food wrappers, empty coffee cups, wadded kleenex, week old newspapers, golf clubs, and my gym bag. And, that's in the winter. When summer arrives, add a few soft drink cans, empty water bottles, a tennis racket, and golf shoes to go with the clubs.

Please do not call me sloppy, lazy, uncaring, disheveled, unkempt, or dirty. Call me comfortable, relaxed, sensible, realistic, and satisfied. And, do not expect to see me at the drive thru car wash in the winter.

The first warm weather in April will be a perfect day to wash my car with a hose and bucket of soap and water while parked in my driveway.

The Wildcat Creek

It flows in a meandering direction with its relaxed current heading from east to west as it bisects the city of Kokomo. Indeed, the community is divided by what is referred to as the north and south sides, determined by the fixed location of the creek.

My house on South Jay Street was located a distance of two blocks from the Wildcat Creek. Accessible from both my cousin's backyard and the above water trestle used for the Pennsylvania Railroad tracks north of their intersection across East Vaile Avenue, the banks of the Wildcat Creek were a familiar warm weather playground and adventure zone for my neighborhood friends and me during our adolescent and preteen days.

I am unable to recall the circumstances of my first visit to the south bank of the creek. Likely, my age would have been around 9 years old when I embarked on my first curious exploration of the tempting terrain.

The huge vertical structures that supported the trestle were surrounded by a belt of large stones protruding from the surface of the water. We would climb and scurry around those jagged stones, pretending to be marine life adventurers. The visibility in the water allowed us to see catfish swimming in the current, and an abundance of crawdads near the base of the rocks.

We would bait our simple cane poles with worms or the pinchers pulled from the bodies of crawdads and drop rather than cast our fishing line onto the creek. Occasionally, we would hook a fish, too small to keep, and return it to the water from which it had been pulled seconds before with only a modest level of instinctive resistance.

There were occasional hot summer days when my neighborhood band of youthful adventurers would erect a tent along the bank of the creek, and remain for the entire night until the sun reappeared in the morning sky. Sometimes we would take a hike in the darkness of night with the illumination of flashlights guiding us. This was not a lifestyle for the timid or frightened child.

Of course, we were a collection of boys only, no girls allowed under any circumstances. I had no girls included among my circle of friends until the spring of my 7th grade year when the advent of hormonal changes sparked an unexpected interest in Becky and Marsha, nearby neighbors on Jay and Harrison Streets.

That's another story to be told. Before the change in the pitch of my voice and the appearance of light facial hair upon my entry into puberty, my preference to conversation with Becky and Marsha was a visit to the south bank of the Wildcat Creek.

My Parents Were Only Humans

A moment of great awakening occurred, which actually was very gradual and not instantaneous, with the discovery or realization that my Mom and my Dad were only humans.

Their specialness was the fact that they were my parents. Otherwise, without intending to diminish or to discredit their importance, they were just two rather ordinary people adding to the population of our planet during the years of their lengthy lives.

Simply, since I am not a member of any special class of humans it seems logical to conclude that my parents, too, justly deserve classification among the ordinary members of our human species.

But, it is that very ordinariness which marks their uniqueness. Being bequeathed by the inheritance of their biological nature with all of the instinctive flaws of our common humanity, their modest achievements are remarkable.

My parents were good, honest, solid, and simple people whose lives modeled for us an exhibition of kindness, empathy, tolerance, and generosity. Their achievements did not rely upon substantial savings or earnings, a trophy house or spouse, or public acclaim. They lived quietly and without fanfare or public recognition. But, their anonymity did not diminish their worth.

After the death of my Mom in 2009, my ongoing relationship with my Dad until his death in 2013 most resembled the bonds of best friends rather than father and son.

As he approached the inevitably of his death, he revealed his humanity to me, conversing about his childhood, regard for his father, his protective mother, his departure from Italy, ocean voyage, and arrival in America, alone, at age 17, and the brutality of warfare witnessed by him on World War II battlefields in Europe.

My Mom was a person of genuine kindness who also was a person with a keen intellect. Reluctantly, she was forced by the harsh economic conditions of the Great Depression to discontinue her formal education at age 16 and instantly seek employment toiling on an assembly line in a local factory.

She was smart but also she was a devoted housewife who felt it her solemn duty to make a comfortable home for her spouse and children rather than being allowed to pursue a professional career.

Maybe the best we can do in our brief and abbreviated lives on earth is to promote the inspirational thought that we humans need no excuse to justify our being alive, that the demonstration of simple acts of kindness, honesty, empathy, and love confirm the worthiness of every human life.

Empathy

Do you find it difficult to help another person who appears to be in great financial need? Most of us have a reflex reaction to the plight of others where our default response is to look the other way. To paraphrase Mr. Scrooge and his abrupt reply to the gentlemen seeking a collection for the poor, do we not have proper charities to care for the needs of the unfortunates among us?

The most satisfying emotion in life is the joy that accompanies the act of helping others. Everyone knows someone who is struggling to afford the monthly mortgage or rent payment, put groceries on the table, purchase fuel for the car, and during the festive holiday season, buy presents for the children in the family.

It's humiliating and costly in terms of a person's self-esteem to beg for charity from others. However, when a gift is given without being requested it is not the product of begging but a pure display of human kindness delivered without creating any obligation between the provider and recipient.

Identify that person, that child, or family whom you know to be suffering from the effects of financial distress and become an instrument of kindness in that person's life. Buy and deliver a Christmas Day turkey complete with the trimmings and side dishes, toys for the children, and gift certificates for adult clothing, fuel for the car, warm coats for the children, and tickets for a movie at the town cinema.

Do not pretend that you are unable to identify a person in need of your kindness. It might be a relative, an acquaintance, or a neighbor. Despite his or her destitute, distressed, and desperate appearance, he or she shares with you the essence of an eternal soul, the promise of life everlasting, and the benevolence of a loving God.

My Childhood City's Founding Father

It snowed today which seems rather strange since it is April 17th and it should be warm and mild outside rather than cold and blustery. Today's unanticipated weather reminds me of the story of the founding of Kokomo which occurred in the winter of 1842. I wonder if you, too, are familiar with the true story.

Many people mistakenly believe that the founder of Kokomo was a pioneer trader named David Foster. Of course, all of us know that the famed "City of Firsts" is named in honor of a Native American Miami tribal chief formally named Kemo-sabee, later shortened to the simpler to pronounce and to spell name, Kokomo.

The actual founder or first settler in what is today the city of Kokomo was Horace T. Phileas. Here are the facts of the basic story about him. (Also, Horace originated the celebration referred to in our contemporary culture as Halloween.)

Specifically, according to my confirmed research Horace arrived from upstate New York in the middle of winter in 1842 with a mule and wagon and nothing else. Horace arrived near sunset and stopped to rest his mule and to make camp at the site of what became Kokomo. Also, he suffered from a severe right foot bunion which made it very difficult for him to walk long distances and required frequent breaks or stops to occur in his travels.

The very next day after his arrival Horace wisely chose to build a rather primitive cabin for a simple dwelling located along the south bank of the Wildcat Creek near what is today the intersection of East King and South Jay streets.

A once in a century event heavy blizzard greeted Horace upon his arrival. He is reported to have said aloud to himself: "Let's make camp here for the night and stay until the weather improves." Well, 178 years later and the weather has never improved. When Horace died from chronic inebriation in 1857 his cremated ashes were solemnly spread by his grieving widow and children in the flowing water of the Wildcat Creek.

The learning lesson or teaching moment for all of us is Horace turned a sow's ear into a silk purse by building the foundation of what became a flourishing and vibrant city while he waited and waited for the weather to clear.

You can sit in the snow and pout or you can rise up and enjoy the natural beauty of a pristine white snow. Success or failure is the result of what we choose to do with the conditions we are given to work with each day.

Life is as simple as the working of the mind of Horace T. Phileas, after all.

Newspaper Reporter and Columnist

My association with my hometown daily newspaper, the *Kokomo Tribune*, began with my newspaper delivery route to houses in my near south east side neighborhoods at age nine, in 1956. I continued delivering papers on my bicycle until the spring of 1963.

I always have enjoyed creative writing projects. In my elementary school days at St. Joan of Arc, I was the apple of the teacher's eye with my talent for writing original essays. My topics ranged from my dog, Nipper, the art of raising pigeons, playing basketball on my backyard dirt surfaced court, to adventures on the south bank of the Wildcat Creek.

During my first year at Kokomo High School, I joined the staff of the *Red and Blue*, the weekly paper distributed to all members of the 4,000 students enrolled in the high school. It was a very professional product, composed by students, and received many state and national awards for its excellence.

My first year writing for the school newspaper was as an editorial page contributor, occasionally having my submissions selected for inclusion in the printed weekly edition of the widely distributed paper. The next year I was chosen to write a weekly editorial page column, which was a coveted position on the paper's student staff. My last or senior year I was selected to be the editor of the editorial page which allowed me to be the author of the formal weekly student editorials.

After my junior year of high school, I landed a summer job working afternoons in the circulation department's loading dock in the rear area of the *Tribune* building at the corner of Union and Mulberry Streets.

In the evenings that summer, I managed the switchboard and handled the telephone calls from upset customers whose paper had not been delivered by her or his paperboy that day. My job was to sooth and to calm the irate customer and then arrange for a paper to be delivered promptly, by a call either to the carrier whose route included the overlooked house or a city cab to drive and deliver the day's paper to the customer.

At the end of both the summer and my job at the newspaper, I was asked to be the senior editor to be responsible for supervising the development of a page to be included in the weekly Sunday edition of the *Tribune*. The theme would be articles and photos that would appeal to the late adolescent and teen aged readers.

Three other younger high school students were added to the staff of the page which was given the masthead or title of "*Twelve To Twenty*," to emphasize its youthful flavor and targeted readers.

I enjoyed my participation in developing and contributing to the success of the *Twelve To Twenty* page published every Sunday in the *Tribune*. I ceased my role upon my graduation from high school in early June, 1965. We received five dollars ($5.00) weekly as student contributors. Indeed, I have kept for sentimental reasons the first five dollar ($5.00) paper bill paid to me for my work as a writer.

I returned to the *Kokomo Tribune* as its summer intern in 1968. I wrote many features and news articles, and received a national writing award for outstanding performance as a summer intern at a daily newspaper. I was flattered and honored by the announcement of the award and grateful for my receipt of a monetary prize in the amount of Two Hundred Fifty dollars ($250.00).

During my senior year at Notre Dame, I began writing a weekly column in September, 1968, published every Sunday in the *Kokomo Tribune*, titled "Notes From The College Scene." I was paid the sum of twenty five dollars ($25.00) for each submitted column. The last column was written and published in conjunction with commencement Sunday marking my graduation from college in early June, 1969.

After my graduation from college, I received attractive job offers from many national and prestigious daily newspapers. I turned down the offers due to my plans to attend law school or expectation of being drafted for military service. But, during the summer of 1970, I worked as a summer intern at the Washington D.C. *Daily News*. I contributed feature "human interest" articles and greatly benefitted from that experience.

The summer internship in 1970 was the last of my employment as a writer or reporter for a city or metropolitan daily newspaper. However, I converted my interest in writing into a valuable communication tool used daily in the practice of law. I have no doubt that my merging of careers in both law and writing enhanced the profitability and success of my legal career.

Time Travelers

Time intrigues all of us. It also bewilders us, and confuses us, and amazes us. It is present every moment in our lives. Its rapid passage can frighten us, and sadden us. It also can refresh us, challenge us, and enrich us.

Where is that toddler who crawled across the family room floor, who stood wobbly and walked proudly across that same surface, who gave a hug and shared a radiant soft smile as she departed through the family room door on her way to her first day of school, who paraded excitedly with her class across the stage to receive her high school diploma, who combined both sadness and joy on her face as she waved goodbye from the steps of her residence hall at the beginning of her college career?

We must learn not only to accept the inevitably of change but also to enjoy the pleasures which life brings us each day. It is not for us to dwell on what was but to look forward to what will be. Life for us on earth is only the childhood of our immortality.

It is a day of momentous growth in a person's life when he or she, through the empowerment of faith alone, no longer flees anxiously from the prospect of change but instead welcomes confidently those inevitable events which occur in the progressive advancement through the experience of life.

Beginning each day with a private silent prayer, we seek the inspiration to recognize the presence of goodness in a world that often seems filled with only the work product of evil, to believe that there is purpose in our being, to view as we travel along the pathway of life the beauty of a creation that is not intended to be a daily problem for us to solve but a mystery for us to live in harmony with the spirit of life's Creator.

The Rocchio Brothers (And Sister)

My Dad had three (3) brothers also residing in Kokomo, two (2) on a full time basis with their spouses and children, and one (1) a part-time resident following the pattern of my grandfather's cycling between Italy and the United States.

The oldest brother, being the part-time resident, was John, the eldest child and sibling. John's spouse remained in Gallo, and during his periods of residence in Kokomo he lived in a sparse apartment on East Vaile Avenue. Uncle John was a beloved person who often visited our home for coffee blended with whiskey after Sunday Mass, conversing with my Dad in their native Italian language.

Joe was fourteen (14) years older than my Dad. Joe, his spouse, Angela, who also was a native of Gallo, and their children resided for many years on South Ohio Street, adjacent to a neighborhood grocery operated as a spousal endeavor. My Dad had great fondness for his brother, Joe. We would visit Joe and his family on spontaneous or unplanned occasions, and my strongest memory of my Uncle Joe is his broad smile.

My Dad's closest sibling relationship was with his brother, Frank, who was ten (10) years the elder. Uncle Frank, his wife, Maddalena, and their children lived on East Vaile Avenue nearby and in close proximity to my family's residence on South Jay Street.

Often, I would accompany my Dad on a short evening walk to visit Uncle Frank at his house where we sat together on separate chairs under the shade of a single front yard tree until we retraced our steps and returned home.

On many Sunday mornings after Mass, Uncle Frank would join with Uncle John and my Dad at the kitchen table in my house for a cup of rich black coffee sweetened with a shot of whiskey, as they discussed in their native Italian language everyday life events, interspersed with bouts of hearty laughter and copious use of hand gestures.

My Dad's other three (3) brothers were men with whom I had no personal contact. His brother, Tony, died at a relatively young age in 1936 while residing in West Virginia. Both Dominic and Mike migrated to Argentina; the former died in 1965 and the latter in 1990.

The brother with whom my Dad had the closest contact or relationship during his youth in Gallo was Mike, who was only six (6) years older. However, the sibling with whom my Dad was most closely connected was his sister, Rosa, who lived her entire life in Gallo. Rosa was only four (4) years older than my Dad and she acted as his big sister, his guardian angel, and his surrogate mother.

My grandfather, Pasquale, according to a port of entry record, was known affectionately as Patsy. He had four (4) siblings, all brothers. My grandfather was the oldest in his sibling group.

Next in age to my grandfather was a brother named Raffaele, who was born and died in 1874. The next child, six (6) years younger than my grandfather, was born in 1879, and also was named Raffaele. The fourth child was Antonio, born in 1884. The last and youngest brother was Giuseppe, born in 1889, sixteen (16) years after my grandfather's birth in 1873.

Similar to my lack of any direct personal contact or relationship with my grandfather, I never met or spoke with my great uncles, with the exception of the youngest member of the brood of brothers, Giuseppe, affectionately referred to by me as "Old Uncle Joe" to distinguish him from my Dad's brother, Joe. Old Uncle Joe, also called zizzi, the Italian word for a revered uncle, was a treasure to me. Residing in Kokomo, he was a presence in my life from the year of my birth onward until his death in 1970.

Old Uncle Joe, or zizzi, with the exception of winter, would visit Uncle Frank and Aunt Maddalena's front yard like clockwork each evening before sunset, sharing conversation with them in their native Italian language, sitting side by side in chairs which had been removed from the tavern restaurant across the street, owned and operated by Uncle Frank and Aunt Maddalena.

The chrome framed red vinyl covered chairs are visible in my mind's eye. A stiff back, a rather hard seat extending parallel to the ground, two (2) hollow legs at the front of the seat descending to the grass surface, curled and continuing away from the front, connected as a single unified piece of tube placed below the seat and in the rear of the chair.

My Dad, often accompanied by me in my adolescent and teen years, would join his brother, Frank, sister-in-law, Maddalena, and his beloved uncle sitting in those uncomfortable chairs, under a small shade tree in the front yard, enjoying the delight of relaxed conversation. Unfortunately, I was unable to understand a word of the dialectic Italian they preferred to speak when together.

Today, I would sacrifice a treasure to have a conversation with Old Uncle Joe about his brother, my grandfather, Pasquale (Patsy) and their parents, Giovanni and Caterina. I would have a thousand or more questions to ask him. But, when he was alive it never seemed important or relevant to me to have that conversation with him. What lingering regrets I have now for that irreplaceable lost opportunity.

My Dad and his brothers were the generation that walked across a bridge from a familiar life in Gallo to a destabilizing life in America. In fact, two (2) brothers chose Argentina but the other five (5) men selected the United States. They achieved a magic like transformation from their parochial life in a mountainous village of Italy to the diverse culture, foreign language, and radically different environment of a city in central Indiana. And, they accomplished that achievement without forsaking or abandoning their roots in Gallo.

They switched the centuries old attire, their native festivals, and their unique dialect of the classical Italian language for the modern wardrobe, local holidays, and their best effort to speak recognizable English. In a pure way, the Rocchio brothers were true pioneers, ambitiously relocating to either the United States or Argentina.

Fleet Activities Okinawa

After Naval Justice School in Newport, Rhode Island, my class, numbering 72 newly licensed lawyers, was dispersed to their duty assignments, most being in the continental United States.

I drew a short or long straw, depending upon a person's viewpoint, and received orders to report to Commander Fleet Activities, Okinawa, which is and was the largest body of land in the Ryukyu Islands south of mainland Japan.

Okinawa is an island in the Pacific Ocean more specifically located in the East China Sea. It was the scene of some extremely fierce battles fought on land and sea near the end of World War II. Despite the extreme devastation inflicted upon not only building structures but also the native people, most Okinawans always had smiles to greet Americans, having adapted to living in harmony with thousands of U.S. active duty military personnel and their families.

In my years of active duty service, the Navy likely had no less than 250 lawyers in its officer ranks. Probably, half the roster of lawyers was assigned to desks at the Department of the Navy or other bureaucratic offices in Washington, D.C., and its surrounding suburbs.

Perhaps, no more than 15 to 20 Navy lawyers were stationed abroad, on duty overseas, serving with The Fleet. I was extremely proud to be among that rather distinguished group of Navy lawyers. I had daily contact with enlisted personnel, interacted with all types of career naval officers, and was given the opportunity to go aboard numerous ships, including some of the most legendary wartime vessels.

I was the only lawyer for the Navy in Okinawa. As such, I served as the Staff Judge Advocate for Commander Fleet Activities, Okinawa, with overall responsibility for all naval personnel and activities on the island. Indeed, I was the youngest staff judge advocate on active duty in the Navy. It was a wonderful and exceptional experience that made a substantial contribution to my development as both a person and a lawyer.

My tour in Okinawa was for a period of 18 months, from the first week of January, 1973, until early July, 1974. Theresa joined me in Okinawa after she had completed college in June, 1973. During our time together living in the Far East, we traveled to Formosa, Philippines, Malaysia, Thailand, Singapore, and Tokyo.

I usually cheer for Notre Dame when my alma mater plays other colleges in football. However, the exception is that I root for Navy when the midshipmen of the naval academy play Notre Dame in their longstanding football rivalry. Go Navy!!!!

I was relatively "anti-military" when I began my service in the Navy. But, after I had become acquainted with the real people who populate "the navy," my regard for the officer ranks and enlisted personnel changed from negative to positive. There was a kinship in the fleet that was a unique experience for me. Everyone should be so lucky.

Challenging Hypocrisy and Corruption

In my long career as a lawyer, I often encountered situations that were examples of hypocrisy or corruption. Certainly, I had my faults and shortcomings but I always attempted to be authentic and genuine.

Probably because of the tough common sense education I received on the streets of the near south east side neighborhoods of Kokomo during the character forming years of my youth, I was never reluctant about "calling out" institutional misbehavior or cronyism when I saw it occurring in the conduct of others.

The harsh blowback and targeted criticism my words and actions would cause me to experience did not discourage me from taking a stand on principle when I felt it necessary and appropriate.

I battled with school and city recreation boards, local and state officials, biased or rude judges, overreaching regulators of attorney discipline, and the federal bureaucracy, including the Veterans Administration and the Department of Navy.

I also regularly criticized and exposed the indifference to human suffering too often displayed by insurance companies in their denial of legitimate claims for benefits made by and rightfully owed to their policy holders.

Possibly, the most public conflict in which I was involved was with the Attorney Disciplinary Commission appointed by the Indiana Supreme Court. It was widely known by lawyers with an Indiana law license that the disciplinarians targeted only those attorneys who offered legal services to clients either in the setting of a relatively small two or three person firm or in the format of a single person sole proprietorship; I was among the latter category. Large sized firms consisting of many lawyers were off limits and untouched by the regulators of attorney misconduct.

I deliberately chose to battle the Indiana system which was influenced and corrupted by the self-serving interests of the largest in number of partners and politically connected law firms operating in the state.

Again, the state's lawyer disciplinarians made no effort whatsoever to regulate the misconduct of attorneys employed at the so-called "white gloved silk stocking" marque law firms.

The result was an embarrassing overreach by the Indiana Supreme Court when it published an opinion announcing the six month suspension of my Indiana law license. That license had no monetary value since my law office was located in the state of Michigan where my activities were authorized by use of my Michigan law license.

Indeed, in the opening paragraph of its professionally defamatory and factually inaccurate published opinion, the Indiana Supreme Court bluntly acknowledged that my "violations" of the code of professional conduct were minimal, normally resulting in imposition of punishment no greater than an informal private letter of reprimand or full dismissal of the matter without further processing being viewed as appropriate or necessary.

My decision to dispute the "charges" was purposeful, intended to engage the Indiana Supreme Court in a process that successfully exposed the corruption and hypocrisy that was caused by its impotent supervision and woeful management of the pompous executive director and narcoleptic members of the state's Attorney Disciplinary Board.

I succeeded in accomplishing my goals and later publicity about the case generated my receipt of hundreds of letters and messages sent by attorneys who expressed their grateful appreciation for my exposure of the corruption present within the Indiana Supreme Court's Attorney Disciplinary Commission.

There are times in life where a person must take a stand on principle, and risk the possibility of incurring adverse consequences resulting from a position of respectful defiance. Shining a bright light on corruption is the best defense society has to the damage caused by the corrosive effects of harmful misbehavior.

Splash of Sunshine

There is something special and majestic about that first warm weather day of a new year. We have been suffering through day after day of bone shivering below freezing temperatures, when suddenly we receive the gift of a day featuring a bright blue sky, a balmy gulf coast like breeze, and the warmth of a brilliant shining sun.

It reminds us that better days are ahead, that nature changes our environment around us, and that human life is dynamic rather than static. Warm days in the midst of a period of severe winter freeze are a reminder that good times can replace bad times with the swiftness of night turning to day.

Possibly, the most basic rule of our universe is the principal of opposites. We find evident in our world the fact that every detectable feature or characteristic has its polar opposite. There is both good and evil, hot and cold, happiness and sadness, hope and despair, joy and sorrow.

Weather reminds us of this truth. If we are suffering in bad times, financially or emotionally, life will change, it will improve, it will be better in the days ahead.

When it seems that every day is just another repetitious day of freezing arctic air, perpetual snowfall, and huge icicles hanging from the roof above our heads, we are greeted in the morning by a splash of sunshine, a wayward bird singing from a branch in the tree, and a renewal of our grateful appreciation for life.

Student Activist

I would describe myself as having been a traditionalist or a moderate conservative politically when I left Kokomo and began my college life at Notre Dame in September, 1965. I also was very unaware of national news and global events involving the United States and both its allies and adversaries.

By the time I graduated from high school in early June 1965, my universe had expanded beyond the near south east side neighborhoods to the entirety of Kokomo. Indeed, Howard County outside the city limits of Kokomo was foreign and unexplored territory for me.

Despite a national scene that exploded in the crises of the divisive Vietnam War, the civil rights movement, violent ghetto riots, and political assassinations, I remained impervious to the tremors that shook and unsteadied the nation.

My apathy changed dramatically in spring, 1969, as I approached graduation day and the conclusion of my college years. I suppose my awakening was fueled by the awareness that I very likely would be drafted for active duty military service and dispatched swiftly to the winless war in Vietnam by midsummer, 1969.

My writings and conversations began to express a deep dissatisfaction with American foreign policy, doubting whether the politicians making decisions about my future had the best interests of my generation in the forefront of their agenda for America. I walked peacefully with my fellow college students through the public streets of South Bend to protest the Vietnam War. I also participated in a silent sit-in demonstration outside the Administration Building to protest overly restrictive parietal rules and censorship of the content of student publications.

I found my self-interests aligned with the lofty ideals of the inaugural Earth Day celebrations held throughout the country on March 22, 1970. That single day awakened my concern for the health of our earth environment and the critical need to combat pollution of our nation's lakes, rivers, and streams.

On April 30, 1970, the United States expanded war activities in Vietnam into neighboring Cambodia. That expansion ignited protests on college campuses throughout the United States. Student announced "strikes" were declared and many campuses interrupted regular classroom schedules to enable protesters to attend anti-war rallies and peaceful demonstrations.

Notre Dame was included on the long list of universities and colleges participating in the student initiated strikes. From the stage in the auditorium at Notre Dame Law School, I delivered an impassioned speech that upon its conclusion there was a burst of applause from the appreciative student and faculty audience followed by an overwhelming voice vote to declare the law school as the very first law school in the country to participate in the student strike.

And, on May 4, 1970, there occurred the killing of four students on the campus of Kent State University in Ohio. The disapproval of the violent actions of the national guardsmen which had resulted in the shooting deaths of four young anti-war student activists was immediate.

During the summer of 1970, while employed as a writer at the *Washington (D.C.) Daily News*, I participated in demonstrations on the National Mall, protests in front of the Capitol, and ultimately was arrested for failure to disperse from a crowd of peaceful protesters around the Washington Monument on July 4; charges were later dropped, and thankfully, do not appear in a permanent criminal record.

My student activism continued during my second and third years of law school but to a lesser degree. I became more "balanced" and less invested in the activities that support the worthy causes of world peace, protection of our earth environment, voting and civil rights, and exposure of political corruption.

Also, my active duty experience in the Navy as a lawyer in JAG softened or broadened my views. I acquired a respect for the people who proudly wear military uniforms, particularly the enlisted personnel, sailors I met and befriended serving on destroyers, cruisers, and aircraft carriers stationed in the western Pacific where I was assigned as the staff judge advocate at Fleet Activities Okinawa.

I, however, have retained the values that were embodied in the peaceful student protests and campus demonstrations that occurred during my conversion from an attitude of selfish benign neglect to responsible activism in the pivotal year of 1970.

No Worries About Calories

This is a rather solemn time of the year when we need to pause and reflect on what is and is not important in our lives. Most of our anxiety is the result of worrying about stuff that really has no significance or importance in the bigger scheme of human life in this universe of bright stars.

Conversely, some of our concerns address real issues, and focus on matters that will impact and affect the quality of our lives. An example is the important matter of Thanksgiving desserts. That is something which should not be taken lightly by anyone in our community as if it is nothing when it clearly is something.

Once a year, on Thanksgiving Day, we should allow ourselves to drown in the pool of gluttony, eat until we cannot swallow the terrifying thought of taking another bite of dessert, with or without whip cream topping. The overpowering commingled aroma of pumpkin, lemon, cherry, apple, and pecan pies, each a freshly baked miracle from the kitchen, oh the wretched sinfulness of it all.

There is no possible way to resist the devilish temptation of delicious fresh baked succulent butter crust pies arranged in an enticing circle on the dining room table for my eyes to lust and my stomach to experience. The plates, forks, the ice cream, and whip cream, all stand ready for my use.

If this be a preview moment of everyday dining in hell, I surrender to the devil and plead with him to reserve me at once a room for eternity, equipped with an oversized oven, giant refrigerator, and a table for one.

Thanksgiving, of course, is about plentiful eating and nothing else. Tender turkey slices, stuffed dressing, delicious peas and onions, sweet potatoes covered with marshmallows, onion smothered green bean casserole, colorful three bean salad, gravy drenched mashed potatoes, steamy hot rolls, soft spread butter, and my dog, Charlie, sitting obediently, tail wagging and tongue salivating at my side.

Does life get any better? Thanksgiving dinner followed by desserts is the apex, the crown, the peak of the mountain of my climb up the slopes of life. It alone is the grand prize that makes worthwhile the drudgery of my life. That is what I believe, for now, until the arrival of Christmas.

Honoring Those Christened Patrick

We fail to properly celebrate St. Patrick's Day in our community. There has never been a proper level of attention devoted to this annual event by the citizens of my hometown. This year we have an opportunity to correct that oversight and get it right.

Certainly, there is someone who will come to mind who is named Patrick. It is not difficult to identify a Patrick (me) somewhere in our community. And, when you have identified that person, generously shower on him expressions of gratitude to celebrate both his presence and his life.

For gift ideas, the word contribution is a perfect word to describe what we need to be doing tomorrow on St. Patrick's Day to honor our local Patrick (me). Let's send gifts in the form of money, bills rather than coins, large denominations rather than small sums, and items and articles appraised as valuable commodities, such as an authentic autographed photo signed by the real St. Patrick (not me).

Throw in a gift certificate, covering all expenses for a spring trip to Disney World, including round trip air fare, ground transportation, lodging, admission fees, food and beverages, and gratuities. But, let's not be cheap about this. Add a side trip to Arizona or Florida for a few spring training games.

You probably have other ideas for honoring your favorite Patrick. Do not hesitate to be creative and deliver to him (me) any valued gifts which you believe properly honor and enrich the life of your beloved Patrick (me).

Remember to wear clothing tomorrow containing a bright shade of shamrock green to display your commitment to this new tradition for celebrating every St. Patrick's Day forevermore, lad and lassie.

Be Patient Dry Thoroughly

Now that February has arrived I need to get real about my recent New Year's resolution. A few days ago I realized that I could not fulfill my pledge.

This year my goal was modest. I had pledged to use in the manner consistent with the intentions of its designer a power air blow hand dryer, the type affixed to the wall in most public bathrooms.

What I have lacked in the past and continue to lack is the level of patience required to stand stationary before the device for the time necessary to allow my hands to dry. I am simply too inpatient to do it the right way.

What I should do is make a belated resolution for the current year which would pledge my commitment to the development of greater patience or tolerance for delay. Why am I in such a hurry, why this sensation that it is necessary for me to rush through life, to get on with it whatever it happens to be, to live life one minute ahead of the minute in which I am alive?

Everything around us seems dedicated to reminding us that we need to be hurrying and rushing through the events of our lives. Is time real? Is it possible to suspend the effect of the clock, the calendar, the push to move ahead of others in line, the impulse to press on the accelerator of my life?

Patience may be the greatest virtue a human can develop in our approach to daily life. The sun rises, the sun sets, the earth spins on its axis one time each day, our planet circles its sun one time each year.

I need to go back again and stand patiently in front of a hand dryer, dry my hands and learn from the experience an important lesson about the pace of life.

Delicious Morning Treat

There are many different ways to eat a bowl of oatmeal but there is only one correct way. Of course, my way is the correct way.

First, oatmeal must be served in an ample or generously sized bowl. There is nothing worse than facing a pile of oatmeal squeezed into the confines of a tight undersized bowl. That will guarantee you a ruined eating experience.

When you order oatmeal in a restaurant, ask for it to be made "extra" hot. Repeat after me: not simply warm or hot, but "extra" hot. A tongue burning temperature assures you that the oatmeal will never become distastefully cold before you have completed consuming the entire contents of your bowl.

Oatmeal must, of course, be accompanied by the necessary and basic condiments. Those include brown sugar, raisins, bananas, butter, and blueberries. Place three or four knife tip loads of butter across the oatmeal and wait for it to simmer. Add a sprinkling of brown sugar, followed by a generous distribution of raisins, blueberries, and bananas placed on top of the sweet brown sugar.

Lastly, pour on the milk but do not create a swimming pool in your oatmeal bowl. Add just enough to convert the texture of your oatmeal into the appearance of a creamy enriched mixture.

Mornings and oatmeal go together like a horse and carriage. You will like it. But, don't take my word for it. Try it. Sometimes you just have to take risks to gain rewards in life.

The Relativity of Time

Can we go any slower? If this line gets any longer, I'll scream. Are you trying to set a record for slowest moving car? Why do I always get behind the person with the largest order at the fast food counter?

Like I have nothing better to do than stand here and wait. If you could speak English we could finish this a lot quicker. Why does this computer take so long to connect? This stupid cell phone is the world's slowest.

You must be kidding. It will take forever to walk there. This is so dumb, waiting like this. If you take another second to make a decision, I will strangle you. Do you have to eat so slowly? Just chew and swallow.

Does everyone in town have to be ahead of me in this drive thru lane? It says express lane, stupid. Who do you know who has the time to do something like that? I can not wait all day for the order. What are they doing in that kitchen?

In the first year of the creation of life, the earth would rotate on its axis every 24 hours, and would complete its orbit around its sun in 365 days. In the year 2020, the earth continues to rotate on its axis every 24 hours, and completes its orbit around its sun in 365 days.

Life cannot be hurried along. Relax. Chill. Enjoy the day. Talk to a stranger. Listen to a friend. Be polite. Say thank you. Open the door and stand aside for the person behind you. Say a prayer. Smile often. Be thankful for your life. Slow down. Be your potential. Feel your soul. Love yourself.

Season of Hope and Renewal

Today is the beginning of the season of spring. We witness during this time of eternal hope the rebirth of Mother Earth. Life on our home planet awakens and dances across a stage in front of our eyes costumed in a radiant sunburst of festive colors. It is good to be of this earth.

In place of winter's landscape of somber browns and solemn grays we have an artist's palette of bright pigments, painting nature in brilliant warm shades of blue, red, yellow, white, and pink. A splash of color replaces the bland emptiness of winter's dark mood. An elegant flower arises from the ground and trumpets to us a message of redemption, a morning blue bird sings a glorious song of spring from its watchful perch upon a branch, and a tree waves its leaves in a lazy breeze.

Earth, we welcome your return to us, your assurance of hope, your message that life exists only in the embrace of the present moment, that my yesterday is tomorrow's day after, that my tomorrow is yesterday's day before, and that only in this day is my life forever more.

We celebrate solemnly our permanent dependence upon your soil from which we reap the crops that we eat for the food that nourishes us, your air from which we inhale the molecules that we breathe for the oxygen that sustains us, your sky from which we gather the rain drops that we drink for the water that quenches our thirst.

You are we and we are you, Mother Earth. Thanks be given to the Omega, to our Creator, to our God. As it was in the beginning is now and ever shall be world without end. Amen.

Giving Thanks

We give thanks this Thanksgiving Day, for those politicians who represent us, the people without power, prestige or influence, for our representatives who care about justice, fairness, and virtue, whose vote cannot be purchased by the money of an influential lobbyist, who lack all concern about the outcome of the next election, who cherish family, and value nature.

We give thanks this Thanksgiving Day for our community, those comprising our family, our neighbors, our friends, and the strangers we see only once in a lifetime but remember for a gesture of simple kindness, who stood aside and politely opened the door to allow me to enter first, shared a smile with me as we waited patiently in a slow moving line, quietly offered his or her chair in a crowded auditorium to an elderly person standing in the back along the wall.

We give thanks this Thanksgiving Day for those people we know who are truthful, value honesty, display loyalty, remain faithful to their spouse, generously and anonymously donate money to feed the hungry and to provide shelter for the homeless, volunteer hours of their private time in completing local service projects, revere the American spirit, and honor the ultimate sacrifice of those who died to protect our freedoms.

We give thanks this Thanksgiving Day to you, God, by whatever name you are called, by whatever form of prayer you are praised, by whatever faith you are worshipped, for providing us with this marvelous existence you have created by your will alone, for giving guidance in the clues you furnish us, for patiently listening to our fears, hopes, pleas to you, and by nourishing us with the grace to accept life as a mystery to be lived not a problem to be solved.

Let us be glad, give thanks, and rejoice in this day.

Dance Hall at Seashore Pool

Today I have been wondering why I lacked the courage to ask a pretty girl at the Seashore Pool to dance with me. I always had a reason to stay where I stood, a safe, unseen, unnoticed distance away from the captivating girls filling the dance floor.

Those repeat episodes of most cowardly behavior were frequent occurrences in my early and mid-teen years, beginning with the season opening day of the popular municipal pool in 1961 and continuing through the end of summer in 1963. Beginning in 1964 I had a string of wage earning mandatory summer jobs that substantially reduced visits to the dance hall at Seashore Pool.

Music at the dance hall was provided by a coin operated juke box stored within a triangular wooden framed closet, equipped with two doors, both fully opened and turned back during the day, later padlocked securely when the pool and its dance hall closed each night.

Those who had the popularity advantage on the dance floor were those who had sisters within a year or two in age. Double that envied unfair advantage given by circumstances of birth to any boy who had a fraternal twin sister available for private dance lessons within the privacy walls of home.

Since my sister was almost five years older and regarded me as a nuisance rather than a peer, my dance practices took place alone, accompanied only by an unseen imaginary partner who, fortunately, always had a compliment for my silky smooth dance moves. At least, that is what I imagined her admiring words spoken to me.

But, dancing with a real girl would be much different than dancing with a ghost partner behind a closed door in the privacy of my bedroom.

I would visit the dance hall, usually in the evening but occasionally in the hot afternoon, stand stiffly with other onlookers lining the east end of the covered pavilion, and think about what could but would never be, an act of fulfillment that would require me to move my stationary feet forward, walk confidently like a teen idol towards my coveted target, being greeted warmly upon my arrival, asking her for a dance, an invitation instantly accepted, her facial expression shyly revealing her delight and disbelief that, wow, Patrick Rocchio had asked her, really and truly, to dance with him! Joy to the world!!!

My stationary feet never moved from their planted position off the surface of the dance floor. I never asked and never got to know what might have been had I found the courage to go forward and seek the prize that always eluded me due to my fear and worry about ---- what?

Those who lived during my era as a teen in Kokomo likely share with me many memories of summer fun at the Seashore Pool. It was a treasure for us, affordably accessed by use of a bargain price season pass. The immodest unavoidable nudity of the bathhouse, the woven wooden baskets used to temporarily store our clothes after changing into swimwear, the chronologically numbered silver safety pins used to identify the location for quick retrieval of our clothes to allow us to dress and exit from the bathhouse.

The acrid scent of chlorine in the foot well that we were required to walk through on the path through the shower room from the bathhouse to the outside pool. The high, wavy, and quick sliding boards; the slick and elusive silver barrel horses that no one could mount; the "diving" piers placed in the shallow water; the gates for entry into the deep water portion for experienced swimmers only; the repetitious announcement at 15 minute intervals, cautioning that "If you can't swim, don't go inside those gates," and, the crowded circular cement island in the middle of the nine foot deep water furnished with two low and two high spring boards for either daring head or safe feet first diving.

Enough. I just looked at my watch and I have only enough time before the end of this uneventful day in a recent string of uneventful days to return to You Tube, and view the scenic third and final episode of my virtual train ride adventure through the glorious Canadian Rockies. I don't recall having any interest in taking a train ride through the mountains, however.

I should have asked her to dance, at least once in my life.

Never My Fault

There has been a never ending controversy about the timing of my arrival or time of birth. The place of my birth was St. Joseph Hospital, in Kokomo, Indiana. The physician who presided in managing the birthing experience for my Mom and me was Dr. George Morrison, who most likely had no specialized training in the field of obstetrics.

In 1947, the husband was not allowed to be present at the moment of his child's birth. The male member of the procreative couple was sequestered in the fabled "waiting room" where he remained until the announcement of the birth of his child. During the stressful wait the average male would nervously pace and consume (smoke) an entire pack of unfiltered Camel brand cigarettes.

When my arrival was announced to my Dad, he almost immediately used a phone available in the waiting room and telephoned my maternal grandmother, Rosie, to relay the good news. She remained adamantly committed to the accuracy of her memory that when my Dad called she glanced at a clock mounted on a wall in her kitchen where her phone was located and observed the time as 11:48 p.m., on the day of June 30, 1947. So, it seems that I was born on June 30 although my birth certificate states July 1, 1947, as the day of my glorious arrival.

After Dr. Morrison concluded his role in the birthing experience for my Mom and me, he proceeded to remove his operating room attire, grab a cup of coffee and a cigarette, and set at a desk provided for physician's to use at the hospital and focus on the "paper work" he was obligated to complete to register date and time of my birth. As he completed the forms, Dr. Morrison, presumably, looked at his watch, noted the time, and entered 12:08 a.m., on July 1, 1947, as the time and date of my birth.

So, it is what it is. I have never had the serene calmness and confidence most people feel with regards to the certainty of their birthday. Is my fate influenced by the month of June, or, is it the month of July? That is a very important distinction. To no avail, in my youth I always pleaded for two birthday parties and two sets of birthday presents to ameliorate the confusion in my life.

The only good thing about this disturbing fact of my life is that whenever I have failed to succeed it is convenient for me to blame the effects of the confusion that persists about the time and date of my birth.

My parents always celebrated my birthday on July 1, although I have felt that grandma Rosie should have been given precedence over mistaken Dr. Morrison. I guess I just have to go on living with this dark and dreary cloud of confusion floating over my head. This is not my fault, anyway.

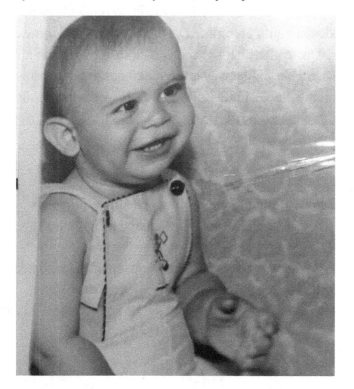

About the Author

The writings of Patrick K. Rocchio are described as being inspired by the "writer's voice," which is a rare gift or talent that enables the author to write in a style that converts the printed word into the spoken voice.

Reading Patrick's writings lifts you into a personal almost intimate setting where the voice of the writer can be heard talking directly to you.

This gift is made possible by the author's use of language (vocabulary, vowels, consonants, syllables, and punctuation) in combination with a cadence or rhythm that creates a flowing melody of words.

Patrick's entertaining and inspirational stories describe those shared features of our humanity that link all of us together into a tight knit circle of family. His stories about life connect on a personal level the ways in which we share the human condition.

Patrick and his spouse, Theresa, reside in a south shore community along Lake Michigan, a few miles from New Buffalo, located in the border crease of the extreme southwest corner of the state of Michigan. They have five adult children and seven grandchildren.

An attorney by profession, Patrick continues to assist disabled clients who live on the edge of poverty, want, and despair. He is valued by those he has helped and he is inspired by their gratitude for his effort.

Patrick was born in Kokomo, Indiana, where he remained residing until graduation from Notre Dame Law School. He served four years on active duty service as a JAG lawyer with the United States Navy. Patrick lived with his family for 26 years in Coldwater, Michigan, and since 2002 he has continued residing on the south shore of Lake Michigan.

CPSIA information can be obtained
at www.ICGtesting.com
Printed in the USA
FSHW011954020620
70810FS